STUNNING HOUSES

WATSON GUPTILL

Author	Editor	Design & layout	Text
Paco Asensio	Aurora Cuito	Mireia Casanovas Soley	*Aurora Cuito:* Introduction, Extension home, Villa Nautilus, Jordi Cantarell House, House and school, Dayton House, House in Lochau, P House, Glass House, Double House, House in Dazaifu, Sendin House, Schickert House, Negro House, Wierick House, Möbius House.
Trarslation *Richard L. Rees*	Copyediting *Juliet King*		*Belén García:* Nirvana House, Cabernet House, House and studio, M House, Bangert House, Byrne House, House in Germany.

Copyright ©	ISBN	Printed in Spain	Editorial project
1999 - Loft Publications s.l.	0-8230-7463-3	Apipe, S.L. Sabadell Barcelona. Spain.	**LOFT** publications Domènech 9, 2-2 08012 Barcelona. Spain Tel.: +34 93 218 30 99 Fax: +34 93 237 00 60 loft@interplanet.es www.loftpublications.com

First published in 1999 by LOFT and HBI,
an imprint of HarperCollins Publishers
10 East 53rd St.
New York, NY 10022-5299

Distributed in the U.S. and Canada
by Watson-Guptill Publications
1515 Broadway
New York, NY 10036
Telephone: (800)-451-1741
(732)- 363-4511 in NJ, AK, HI
Fax: (732)-363-0338

Distributed throughout the rest of the world
by HarperCollins International
10 East 53rd St.
New York, NY 10022-5299

No part of this book may be reproduced or transmitted in any form or by any means electronic or mechanical including photocopying, recording, or by any information storage and retrieval system, without permission in writing from the publisher.

Steven Ehrlich Architects	6	**Extension home**
Hiroyuki Arima	14	**House in Dazaifu**
Pauhof Architects	22	**P House**
MVRDV and Bjarne Mastenbroek	30	**Double House**
David Chipperfield Architects	36	**House in Germany**
Migdal Arquitectos	42	**Villa Nautilus**
Döring Dahmen & Joeressen	48	**Schickert House**
Döring Dahmen & Joeressen	54	**Wierich House**
Dieter Thiel	60	**Bangert House**
Legorreta Arquitectos	64	**Cabernet House**
Vincent James Associates	70	**Dayton House**
Dirk Jan Postel	78	**Glass House**
Kengo Kuma & Associates	86	**House and school**
Tonet Sunyer	92	**Sendín House**
Orefelt Associates	98	**House and studio**
Alberto Kalach	104	**Negro House**
Mario Corea	110	**House in Teià**
William P. Bruder	118	**Byrne House**
Jordi Casadevall	126	**Nirvana House**
Baumschlager & Eberle	134	**House in Lochau**
Jubert and Santacana Architects	140	**Jordi Cantarell House**
UN Studio	146	**Möbius House**
Kazuyo Sejima & Ryue Nishizawa	154	**M House**

We are only a few months away from the end of the century, a century that has witnessed the evolution of the work of prominent architects, in which new technologies have played an important role. Budgetary considerations aside, architecture has no limits and is capable of realizing even the most fantastic dreams of clients, designers and builders. Domestic architecture is a paradigm of this evolution. A privileged field of experimentation, it closely examines the domestic aspirations of our time and places before us new lifestyles and speculations about changes in family, social, and even work environments. Stunning Houses features a selection of homes from the end of the millennium.

This selection looks beyond dictatorial factors like economics, aesthetics or fetishism to examine houses that have broken away from the past and that define today's innovation and tomorrow's classicism. The book does not aim to convert these houses into prototypes or models to follow; they are included because they reflect the peculiarities of their era, sites and owners.

The projects have not been grouped together according to countries or locations. While it is obvious that a house in the high mountains has different requirements than one by the sea, this kind of comparison was ruled out in order to emphasize the characteristics that the featured projects share.

First, respect. Respect for the environment, not in strictly ecological terms, but in terms of how the constructions sit on the land, and how they affect, distort

or enhance the landscape. Also, mutual respect between architect and client, so that the latter's desires might inspire the former.

Second, lightness, as a concept rather than a physical element. Lightness is the result of a determination to eliminate all superfluous elements from the creative process. In the architectural idiom, lightness means clear, direct description, uncluttered by details that make no essential contribution to the project.

Third, appropriateness. Appropriateness in the choice of building materials. Besides determining the tones, light reflection and textures of finishes, materials complete the definitive image of the house and endow the space with a multitude of nuances. Needless to say, materials also determine the durability of the building and its maintenance requirements, affecting practical aspects and, perhaps even more importantly, purely aesthetic ones.

Last, exclusivity. Far from extravagance, exclusivity is implicit in these kinds of projects since they are the products of highly personalized requirements, or briefs. The varying aspirations and limitations of individual future owners lead to a unique project in each case. Furthermore, the architect is given the opportunity to meditate deeply on his creative task, to generate new ideas and to try out new functional or constructional solutions.

The houses featured in the book, though extremely varied, share the common denominator of stunning structural qualities and visual sensations. They are the kind of houses we all dream of inhabiting.

Architects: Steven Ehrlich Architects
Location: Santa Monica, California, USA
Construction date: 1996-1998
Photographs: Tom Bonner, John Linden, Julius Shulman, David Glomb

The Lewin residence in Santa Monica, designed by Richard Neutra in 1938, stands at the foot of a cliff behind Santa Monica Beach in California. Initially, it occupied some 5,920 square feet, to which the present occupants wanted to add a leisure area and swimming pool.

They also required an enlargement of the garage and utility rooms and a re-design of the exterior spaces. The main challenge was to alter a masterpiece of 20th century architecture. The architect's reply was clear: intervention without imitation. The objective was to design a contemporary space of which Neutra would have been proud. The references to the brilliant architect are subtle, and the application of solutions is always personal. This innovative yet respectful allusion to the architect is most clearly seen in the curved roof, which evokes the curves in the plans by the master. The steel structural support is also a reference to Neutra's later work. In order to harmonize with the existing house, an almost monochrome range of colors was used. Prime quality materials (stainless steel, concrete, glazed tiling) set the tone in the extension.

In order to insulate against the noise from the nearby Pacific Coast Highway, Steven Ehrlich decided to place the new garage and utility rooms in such a way as to act as an effective sound barrier, thereby creating a patio common to both parts of the house. As we proceed forward with the road behind us, the next patio we come across also has Neutra's original house as a backdrop and creates a visual link between the existing living room and the new pavilion that contains the leisure area. A glazed bridge crosses this exterior space to unite the two aforementioned zones.

The pavilion, symbolically called the "soap bubble," is covered by a stainless steel cycloid vault, whose inspiration came from the one Louis Kahn used for his Kimball Art Museum in Fort Worth, Texas. Like Neutra, Steven Ehrlich set out to emphasize the interior-exterior relationship; thus, three of the pavilion walls are entirely transparent. The glass panels at either end of the vault slide until they are totally hidden between two bare concrete walls. This scrupulous design gives the complex a luminous, sophisticated air. The southern face of the garage (the one furthest away from the existing house), the utility rooms, and the pavilion are all covered in concrete molded on-site. These elements contain the installations and communications: kitchens, bathrooms and stairs that connect the main spaces.

The Pacific, framed by a large opening in the wall that borders the site, forms the end of a visual axis aligning the pavilion and the swimming pool. The result is a magnificent view of the ocean. The stainless steel door at the end of the pool opens automatically by sliding behind the concrete wall. The new technologies applied here to mechanisms and materials exemplify Neutra's idea of fusing interior space with the landscape in a way that was inconceivable in his day.

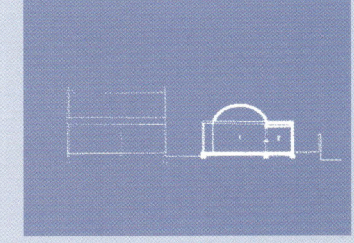

The extension of the Lewin residence is a successful combination of bold choices and the outcome of deep reflection on the work of Richard Neutra. Meticulousness both in the overall planning and details makes this project a uniquely elegant and comfortable residential space.

Home extension

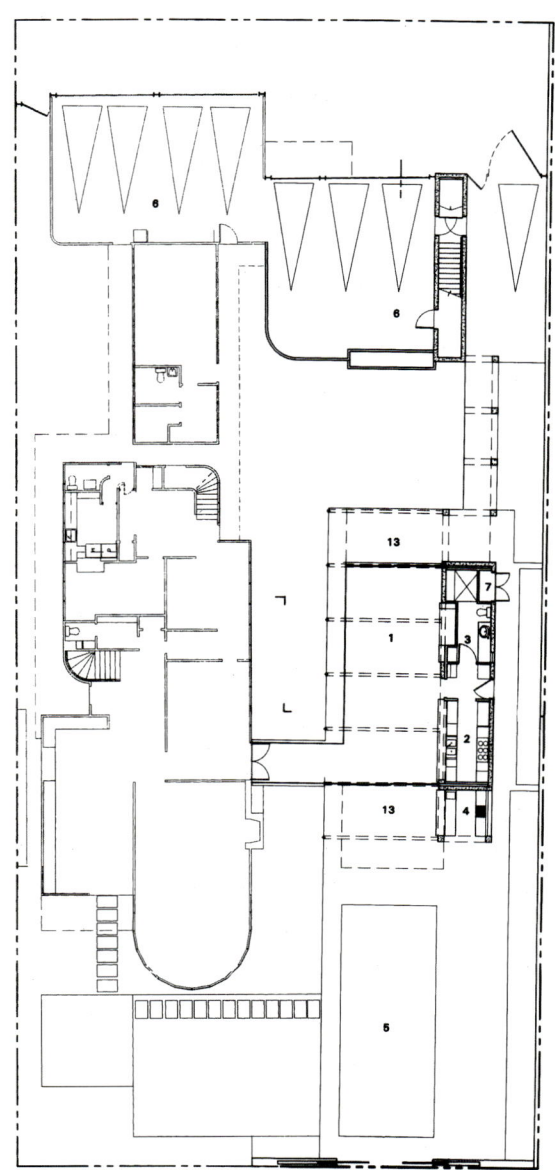
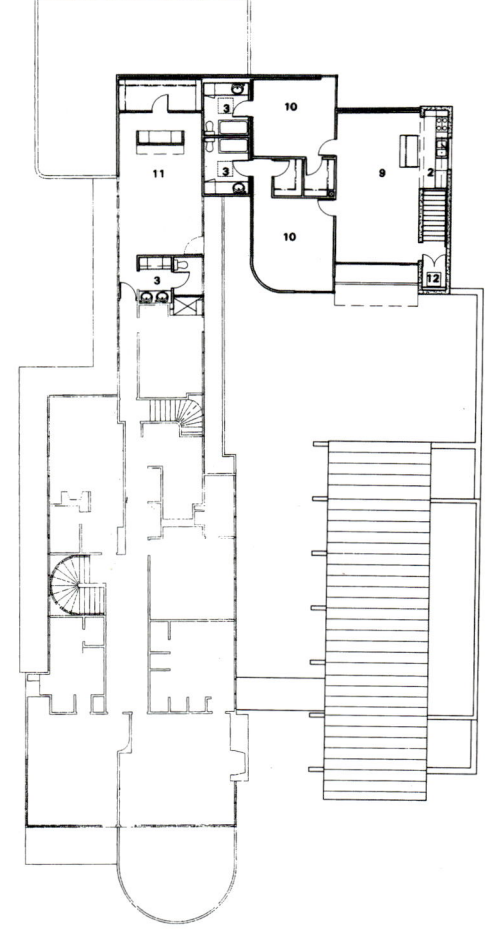

First Floor.

1. Leisure room
2. Kitchen
3. Bathrooms
4. Barbecue
5. Swimming pool
6. Garage
7. Storeroom
8. Entrance
9. Living room
10. Main bedroom
11. Guest bedroom
12. Laundry
13. Terrace

Second floor

Following page:

View of the entrance, designed entirely by Ehrlich Architects, that substitutes the original one, which was much smaller since Neutra's garage needed to provide space for only one car.

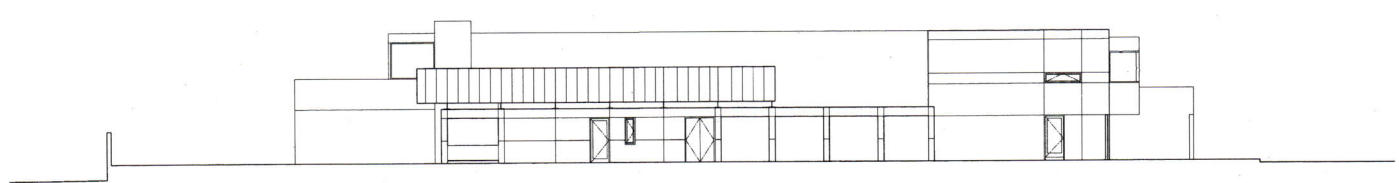

Home extension 9

Living room of the original house connected to the extension by way of a glazed bridge.

View of the swimming pool with the Pacific Ocean in the background.

At night, the lighting in both sections creates different atmospheres, although the overall effect is homogeneous.

Steven Ehrlich based his project on the clear decision to relate to, but never to imitate, Richard Neutra's work. He created genuine forms that evoke the original building. Ehrlich's strategy placed his new construction near the existing house, though not backing onto it. Thus, he created two independent constructions that form a single complex.

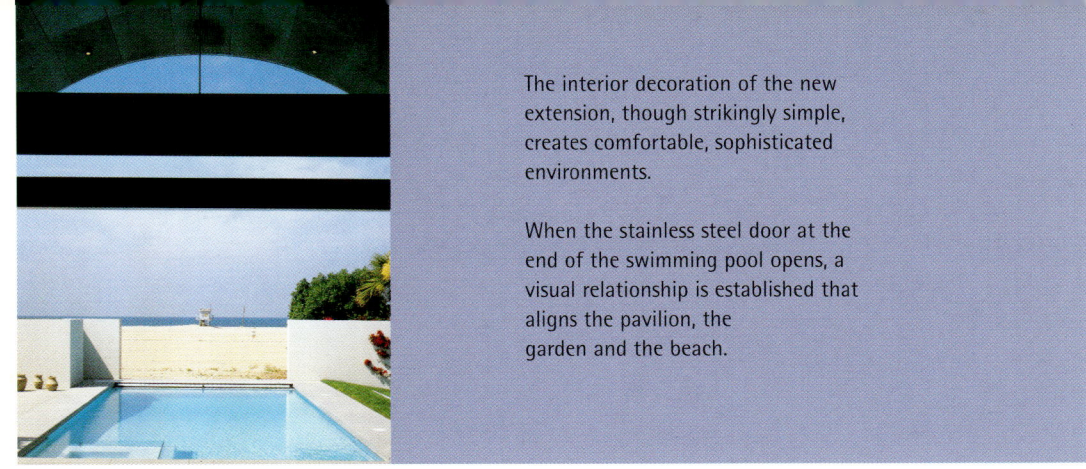

The interior decoration of the new extension, though strikingly simple, creates comfortable, sophisticated environments.

When the stainless steel door at the end of the swimming pool opens, a visual relationship is established that aligns the pavilion, the garden and the beach.

Architect: Hiroyuki Arima
Location: Dazaifu, Japan
Construction date: 1995
Photographs: Koji Okamoto

Japanese architecture is the visual expression of the dichotomy inherent in a unique cultural environment. Futurism, both aesthetic and functional, is deeply influenced by an ancestral tradition that enriches projects with an exquisite sensitivity that is absent from Western architecture.

The most radically avant-garde buildings seem to anticipate the future while remaining faithful to a millennial culture. Although the resulting spaces are bare, minimalist and cold, they are carefully designed and built with specially treated materials. Hiroyuki Arima is a product of this cultural environment.

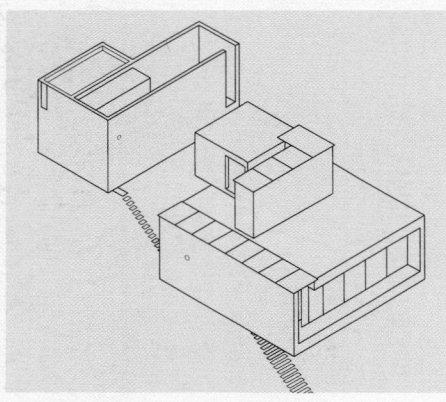

Here, the architect proposes a house that sacrifices functional aspects for full enjoyment of landscape and light. It is a radical project that seeks total links between interior and exterior, a relationship both visual and real. Nature is brought into the house through interior vegetation, natural ventilation and so on.

The house is noteworthy, not for its functionalism or practicality, but for the way it has allowed nature to play a role.

Loyal to this priority, Arima stands apart from end-of-the-century Japanese housing trends, which give priority to obtaining maximum profitability from built surfaces. This project's goals have nothing to do with either economy or getting the most out of the space. The objective is the perception of spaces especially designed to delight the senses. Although the house stands near the Temple of Dazaifu, its surroundings are sufficiently isolated from the hubbub of the tourist area to provide peace and quiet. Bamboo and other autochthonous trees cover the gentle slopes of the site.

The house is divided into two blocks on the slope, the bottom end of which is about thirty feet below the top. From the lower volume, it is possible to enjoy the wide range of views of the Dazaifu hills. Visual perception on this level plays the leading role, since the different exterior frames create the interior atmosphere. This floor consists of a single room containing "boxes" that act as living units.

These units accommodate the different functions of the house: the kitchen, a bedroom and a bathroom.

The volume above, whose limits with the exterior are more sharply defined, is reached by way of a path. This level accommodates a garden enclosed by perimeter walls and a living room that the occupants can modify by shifting the movable partitions.

Apart from the meticulous treatment of constructional details (radically simple carpentry, light inlets at strategic points and sculptural stairs), the project features almost sensual finishes that complete a home designed so that the occupants may enjoy a wide variety of views and nature in all its splendor.

House in Dazaifu

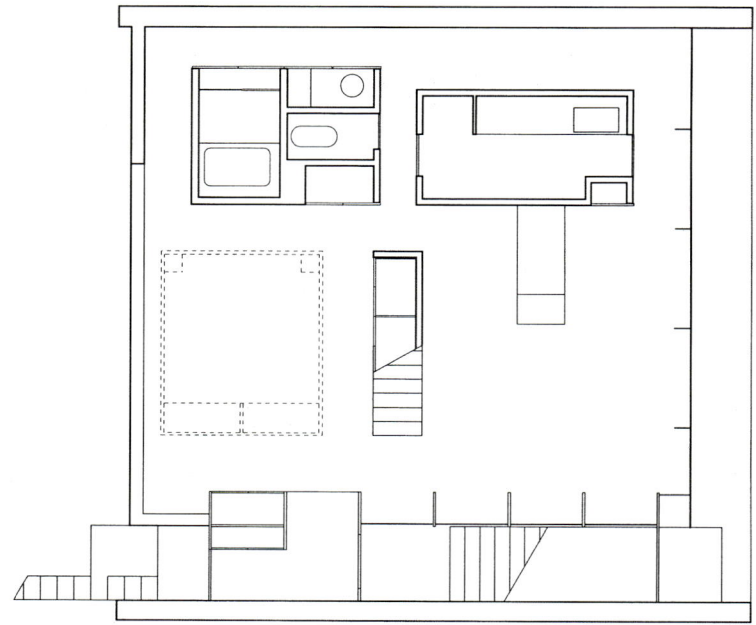

The lower floor is a large space containing "boxes" that include a bedroom with its corresponding bathroom, the kitchen and a living room. Even though this arrangement is detrimental to functionalism, its purpose is to take maximum advantage of the views.

The floor above contains a music room, living room and an open-air patio. Both levels are independent from each other and are linked by a path that follows the steepest slope on the site.

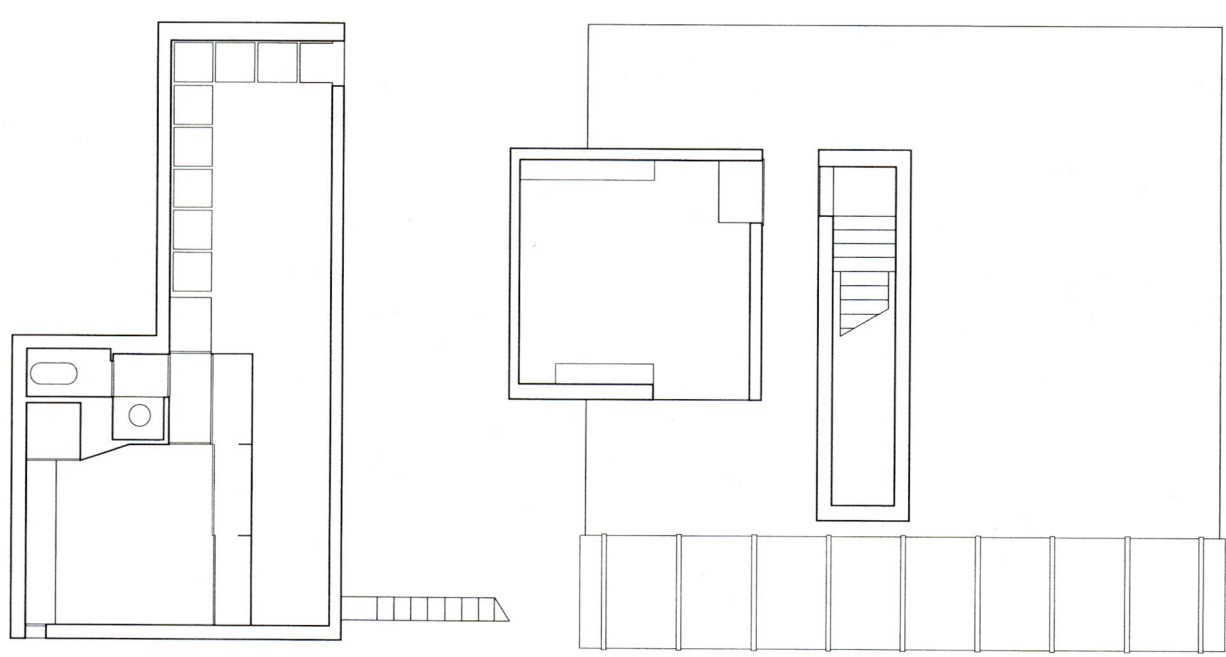

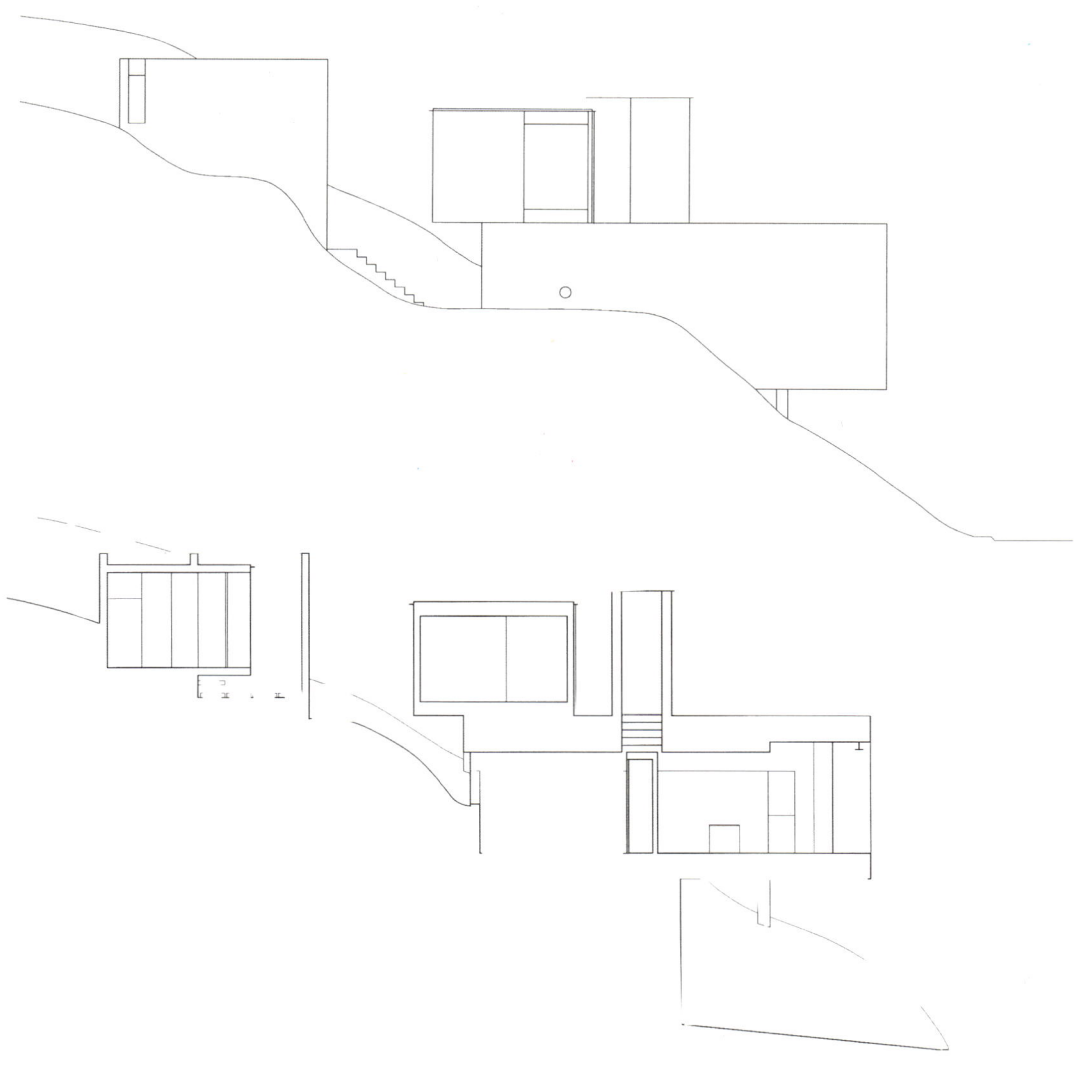

Hiroyuki Arima and his studio, Urban Fourth, have managed to obtain spaces closely linked to the exterior. Their aim was clear: to incorporate light, views and wind into the rooms. Nature slips in either physically or visually through each of the openings.

Elevation and section of the house. The steep slope determined the position of the floors on different levels, which are linked by stairs and paths.

The stairs have been meticulously designed. Like a metaphor, each step has a direct view of the sky. The topmost steps are translucent, allowing light to pass through from above.

There is little privacy due to the absence of curtains or blinds. Certain aspects had to be sacrificed in this project in order to maximize views and introduce natural elements.

Architects: Pauhof Architects
Location: Gramastetten, Austria.
Construction date: 1993-1998
Photographs: Matteo Piazza

This single family home in Gramastetten, designed by architects Michael Hofstätter and Wolfgang Pauzenberg, is located in the Austrian countryside among rippling cornfields with the occasional clump of trees and Mediterranean-like hillsides in the background.

The project is the result of a process of stylistic reduction in a human habitat, which may be understood only as the result of another, extremely delicate and emotionally traumatic process. This explains the feeling of discomfort that overcomes observers when they contemplate the house and attempt to decipher the criteria governing an architectural system of minimalist lines and surfaces.

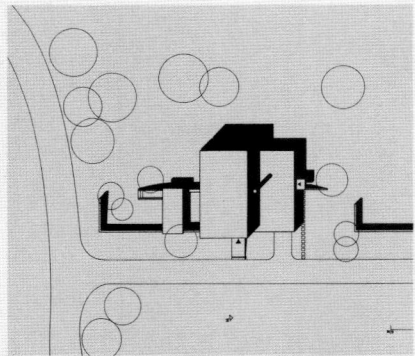

The apparent simplicity of these geometrical forms conceals the difficulty involved in creating a complex system of interior and exterior spaces, separated only by thin partitions and carefully placed screens. The radical reduction of geometrical forms appears to create, on one hand, stylistic proximity to the most refined simplicity and, on the other, an infinite number of possible points of view from which to discover a highly complex design.

The house may be seen as a volume formed from two blocks. One is polished and ethereal, with invisible supports and aluminum plate coverings. This block seems to levitate over its larger, heavy, rough, naked concrete counterpart below. The blocks share the elements of a conventional residential program: the first accommodates the bedrooms while the second houses the living areas and services. The one above is oriented east and west; the one below toward the south. This interplay between opposites defines a project that shuns the typological and linguistic stereotypes of Austrian rural architecture. The consequential bureaucratic obstacles were overcome by sheer tenacity.

There is no physical contact between the two elements. The metal box, which does not actually touch the ground, is anchored to the ground by a concrete wall and supported by a central pillar and wall, underpinned by slender metal supports. Together with the pergola, it limits the exterior space and ensures the privacy of the occupants.

In contrast to the simple, monochrome exterior, the house's interior surfaces have been designed to create a warm, pleasant atmosphere. The arrangement of openings and the horizontal, floor-level light produced by the two overlapping volumes add to the sensation of comfort. The greatest achievements of the P house are the choice of materials, the subtle control of articulations, textures and details, the way the project is implanted onto the landscape, and the permeability between interior and exterior. The project won the Oölandeskulturpreis in recognition of the precision of the work and its fidelity to the original design.

P House

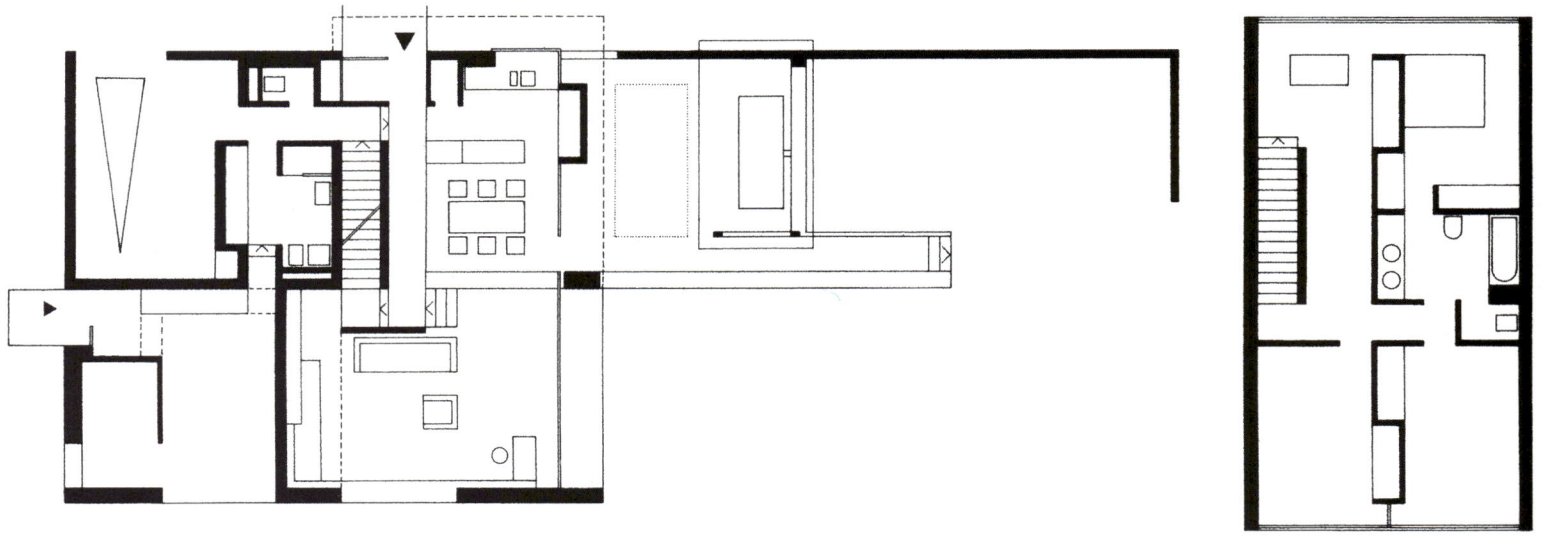

The house consists of two blocks that together constitute the program of a conventional family home. The lower floor accommodates the living areas and services, while the bedrooms are on the floor above.

Elevations of the house. The ground floor is oriented toward the south and the bedrooms toward the east and west. This interplay of opposites is far removed from typical Austrian rural architecture.

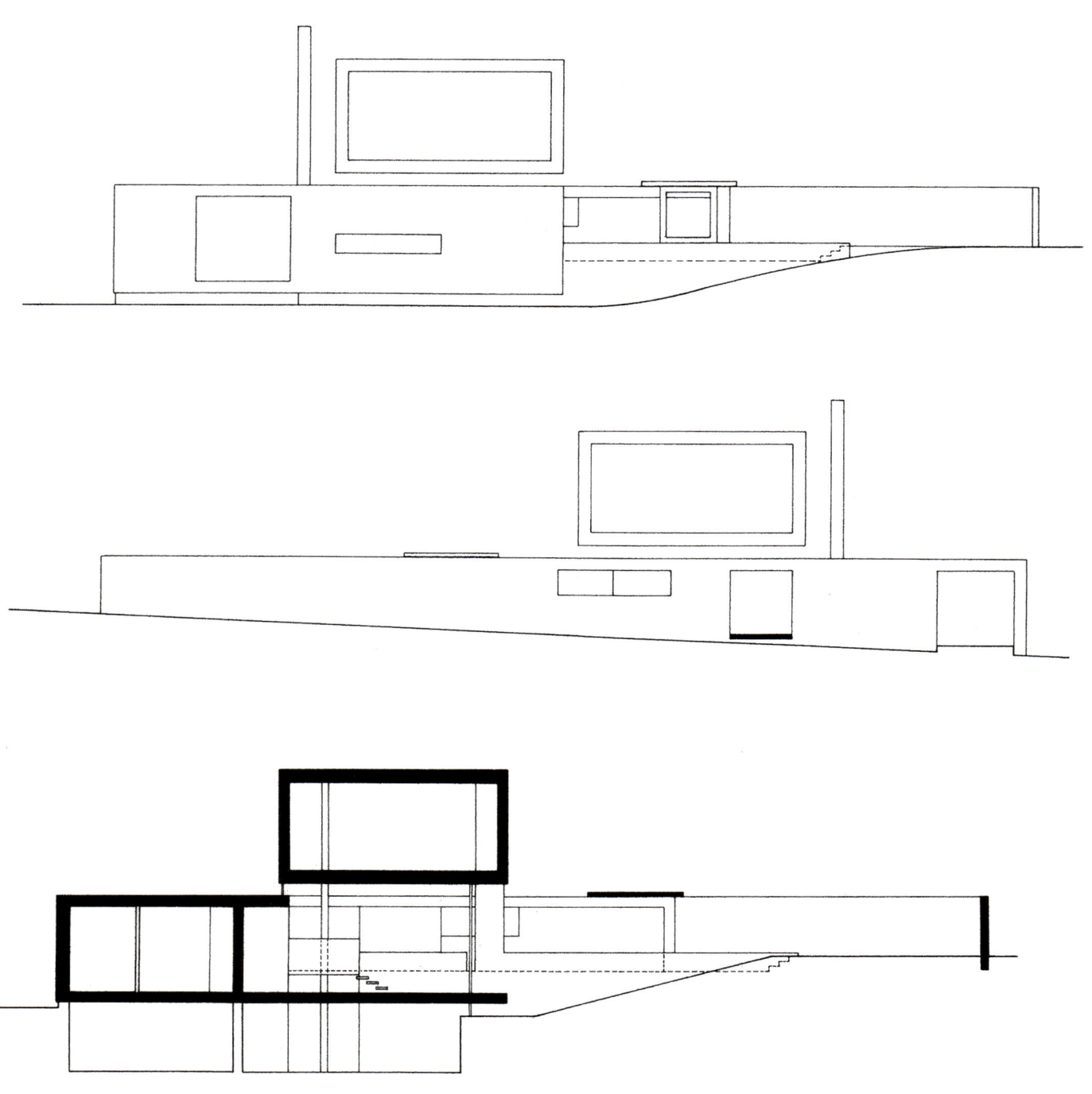

The project involves radical stylistic reduction, the product of a meticulously conducted minimalist process that pares forms down to their simplest expression. The choice of materials determines sober, elegant aesthetics.

From the section we appreciate the differentiation between the two floors, which even avoid physical contact. The second floor rests on a central pillar and a wall that incorporates the stair. Similarly, the floor below has no contact with the ground.

In contrast to the sobriety of the facades, the house interior is warm and welcoming, materials and textures having been chosen to enhance this effect. The way the twofloors are staggered allows light to penetrate at floor level.

Architects: Bjarne Mastenbroek and MVRDV
Location: Utrecht, The Netherlands
Construction date: 1997
Photographs: Christian Richters

The Double House stands on the street that circles a magnificent 19th century park on the outskirts of Utrecht. It is inhabited by two families who share the same building, a three dimensional assemblage that had to reconcile the different lifestyles and needs of the two owners.

Given the difficulties involved in financing an individual construction, the couple who bought the site sought and found another owner with whom to share it. However, it turned out that they did not share the same ideas about their respective future homes, and they separately engaged the services of Bjarne Mastenbroek and MVRDV.

As with their other projects, MVRDV opted for restricting the variables that intervened in the project in order to operate with clarity in this complex situation. Having produced a considerable number of layout plans, they decided to reduce the depth of the dwelling in order to obtain more open air space and increase the surface area of the garden. Thanks to this strategy, physical presence, spatial possibilities and park views were gained.

The house is a slim, protruding piece. Thus, the section displaces the ground plan as the battlefield on which to spatially define and adjust the two homes. The wall that separates them is like a frontier to be negotiated, and is designed as a uniformly thick surface that divides the families' activities.

Consequently, two interdependent houses were created, each one in part the product of the lifestyle and whims of the occupants next door.

The couple living in the larger of the two houses wanted the living room and kitchen away from the street; the other couple placed their kitchen and dining room on the ground floor, while their living room is on the second floor, between the bedroom and the living room of their neighbors. Both common areas enjoy splendid views of the park.

Except for the bedrooms, closed volumes that seem to float in this labyrinthine space, practically every room looks out through glass. In this way, private activities are immersed in public ones, which exemplifies the progressive blurring of the limits between both domains.

Negotiation leading to joint awareness is the central theme of the project. The house highlights the individuality of its occupants and responds to the demand for homes that go beyond conventional or tacitly accepted forms.

Mutual dependence threatened to paralyze all formal and conceptual progress. Though paradoxically, both architects and clients demonstrated that the result is much more effective than it would have been if both neighbors had worked on their own.

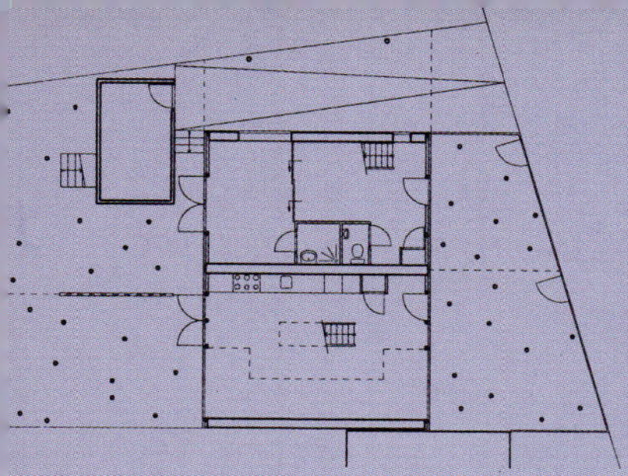

Double House

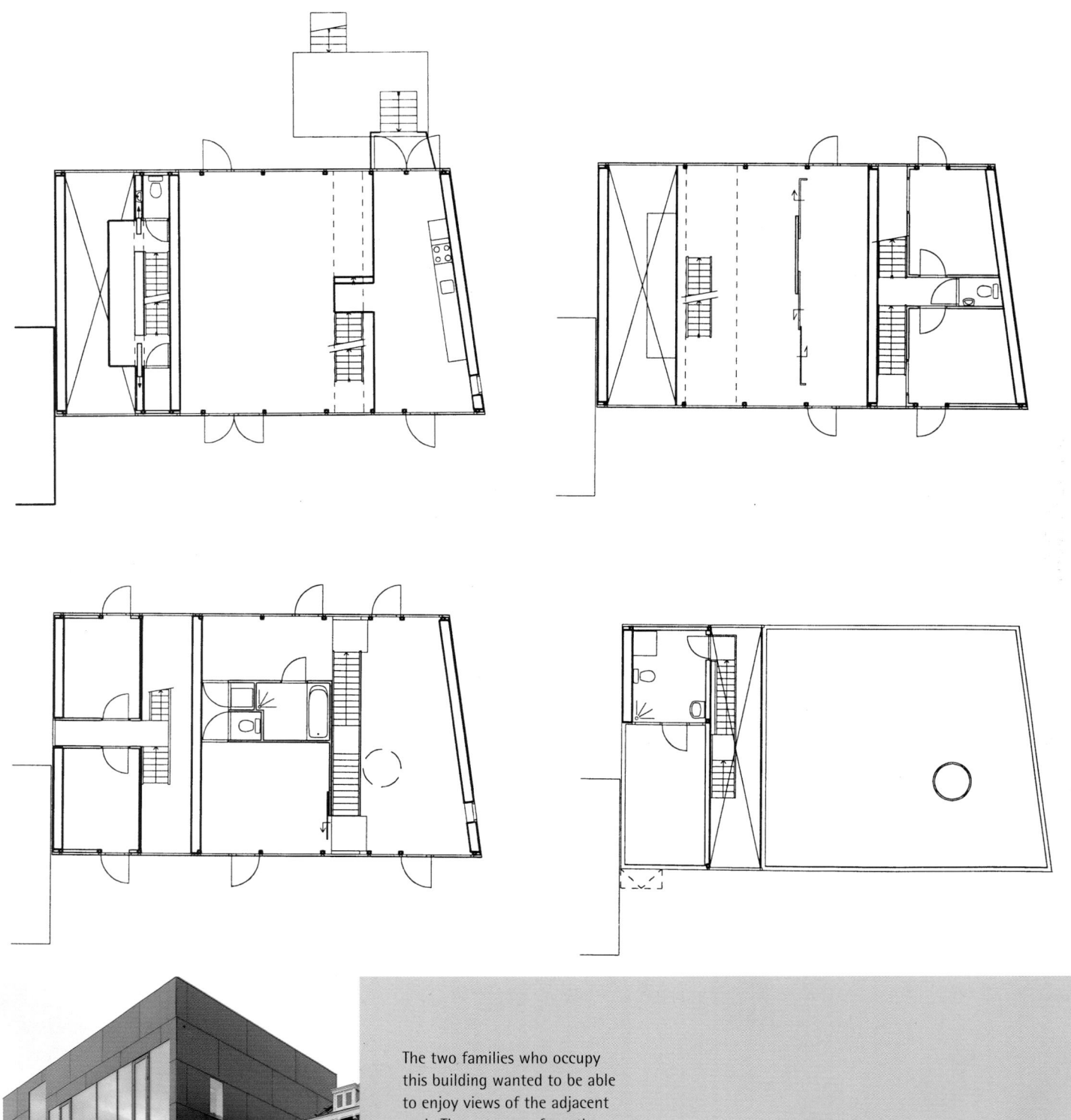

The two families who occupy this building wanted to be able to enjoy views of the adjacent park. The entrances from the street toward the garden and the terrace had to provide free-flowing movement.

The architects designed a house of minimum depth. Consequently, it stands five stories high, leaving as much space as possible for the garden.

Double House

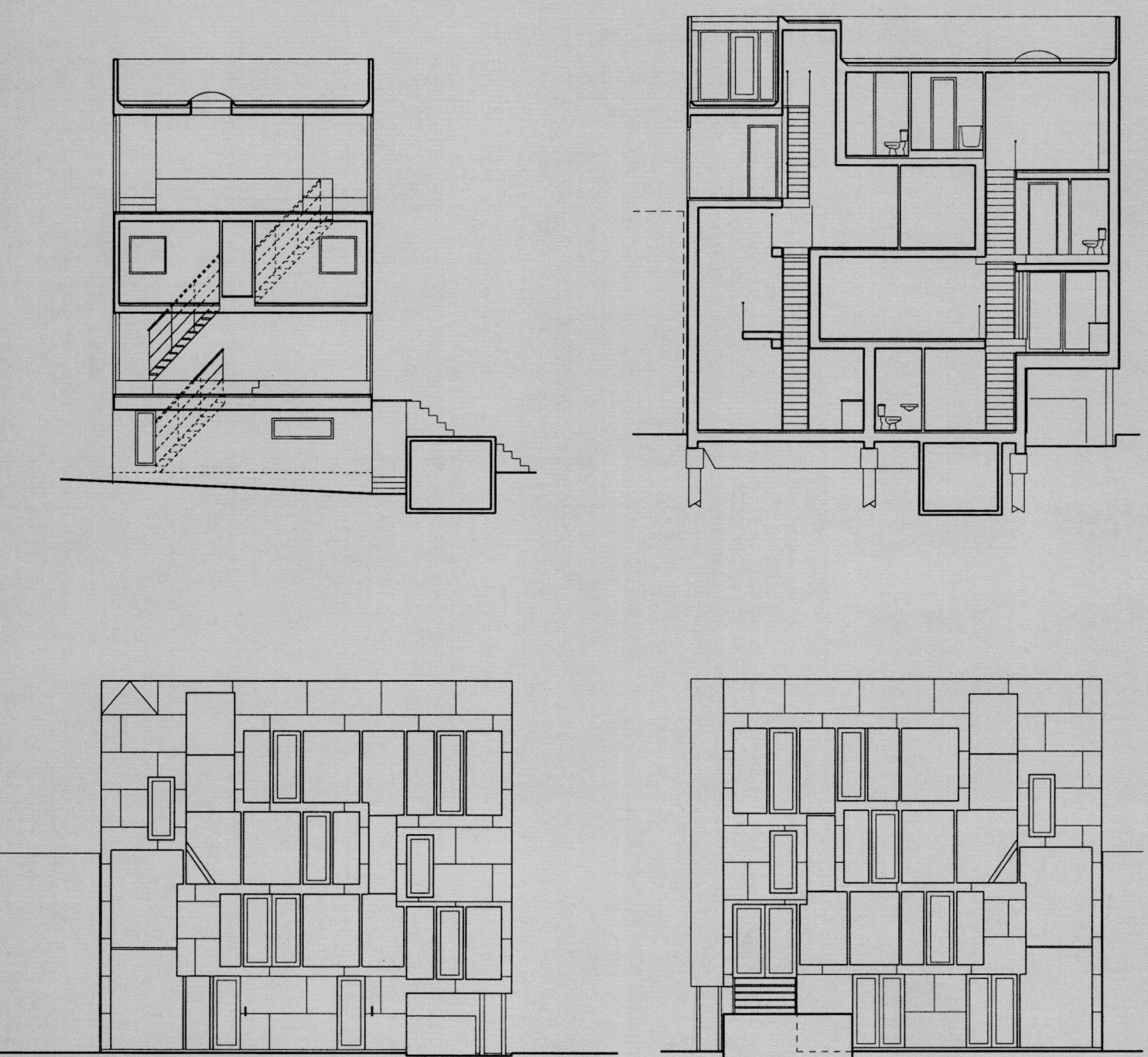

All the rooms together create a labyrinthine structure that horizontally and vertically links spaces pertaining to both families. Except for the bedrooms, all rooms have glazed facades. In this way, the frontiers between private spaces and the exterior are progressively blurred.

The strategy of interior distribution was designed to create flowing spaces. Pillars and the vertical coincidence of walls were eliminated, and the concrete structure transmits the loads diagonally.

Architects: David Chipperfield Architects
Location: Germany
Construction date: 1997
Photographs: Stefan Müller

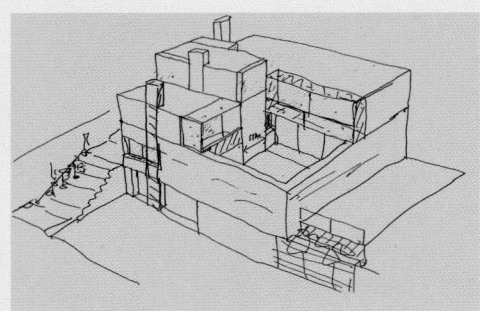

This house is located in a residential zone. Access to the site from the street is gained at the lowest level. The exterior space we first encounter features a naked brick staircase on one side that transversally crosses the site until it reaches the rear garden, leaving behind the side facade with the main entrance.

The architect carefully studied the three-story section of the house. The bottom level, which absorbs the slope of the terrain, is characterized by its meticulous implantation on the site and the treatment of both the interior and exterior. The two floors above are arranged introspectively around a patio oriented toward the rear garden to the south and accessed from the intermediate level.

Chipperfield envisioned this project as a progressive succession of spaces. The house groups together a series of rooms, each one treated individually in terms of both space and composition. The building is designed in three dimensions and attention has been paid to the needs of each room. Such care is evident in the type and size of openings, the ideal heights and the relationship with the exterior and the other rooms.

Two solutions are worthy of special mention: first, the patio as an element around which the program's fundamental applications are grouped; and secondly, the staircase as a piece that unites by simultaneously communicating and separating the different zones on each level.

At the lowest level, the staircase splits the floor into two halves. At the middle and top levels, the position of the vertical nucleus substantially reduces the distribution surface area, thus achieving an ideal connection between spaces.

The house exudes a feeling of intimacy. When deciding where to place windows, the architect took the occupant's point of view, and this is why the spaces are both well related to the exterior and visually protected from one another. The facade overlooking the street is practically blind on its two upper floors that are visible from beyond the site. The facade gives the building an introspective character by isolating it from the exterior in favor of interior landscapes, the patio and the rear garden.

For Chipperfield, materials are crucial elements in this kind of project. Here, he found the texture he wanted in hand-made brick.

What would have been bearing walls — an impossibility due to German building regulations — were eventually built with a feel that is present throughout the house.

Chipperfield also pays special attention to the combination of materials. Alongside the irregularities of hand-made brick are large surfaces of glass and steel that create a duality that might be interpreted as a criticism of contemporary attitudes, the trends toward both perfect finishes and the neutralization of materials.

With this project, the architect has managed to combine careful attention to the site and the wellbeing of the occupants with a variety of mental mechanisms, such as abstraction. In short, Chipperfield is a worthy sustainer of central European traditions — in which Mies and Mendelsohn would be two possible references — of late 19th century and early 20th century domestic programs.

House in Germany

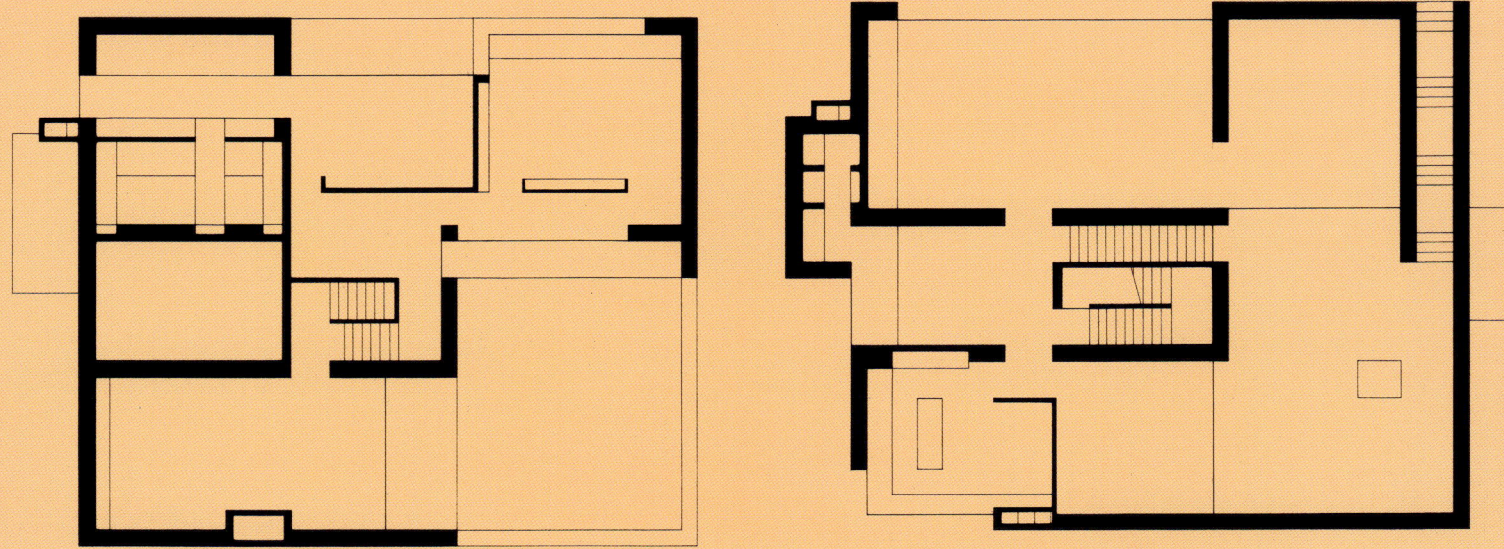

The aesthetics of this house are characterized by the contrast between the glazed surfaces and the roughness of brick. This deliberate conflict between irregular materials and perfectly smooth surfaces may be seen as a criticism of current trends toward perfect finishes.

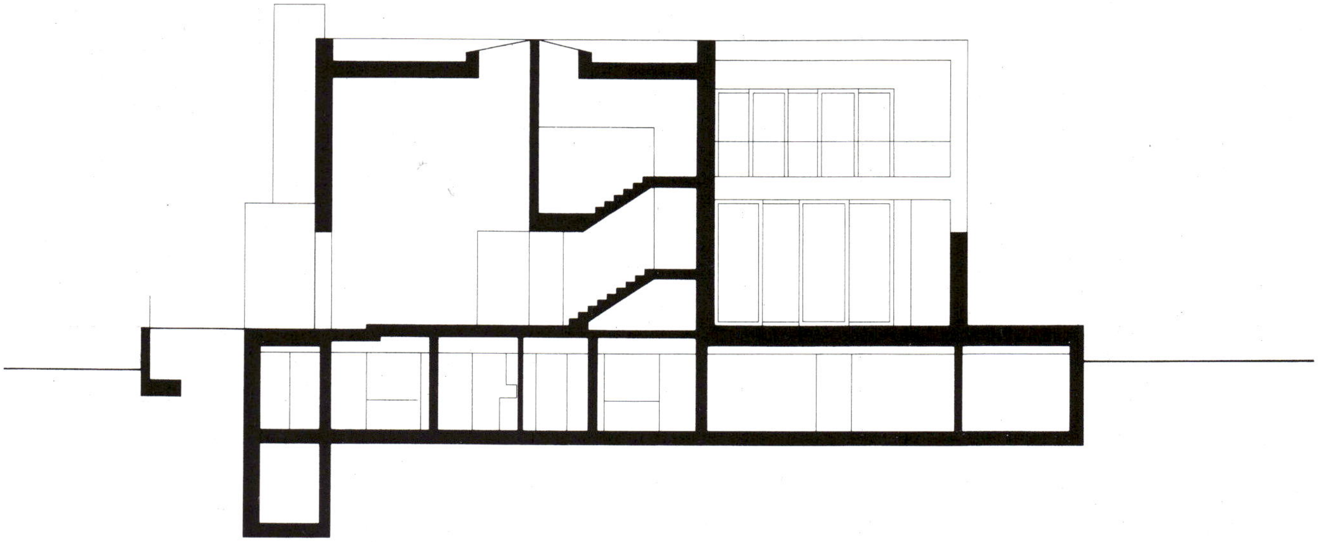

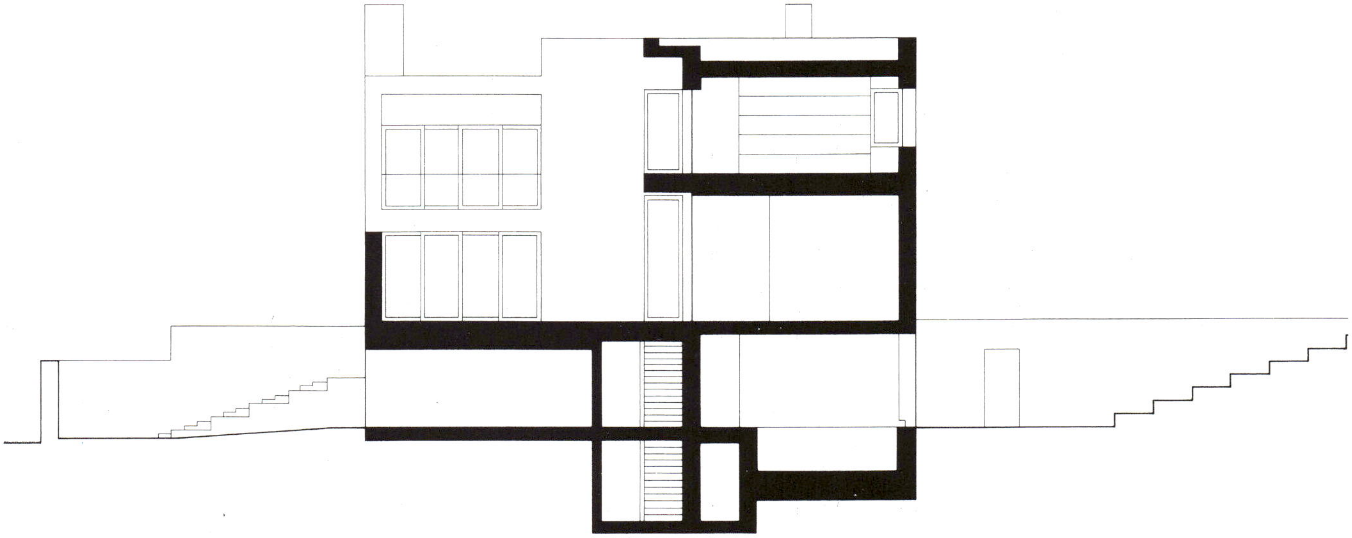

The spatial composition, which was studied in three dimensions, features several levels and ceilings at different heights. This vertical contraction and expansion of the building may also be observed on the facade, where there is an obvious interplay between physical constriction and abstract freedom.

Architects: Migdal Arquitectos
Location: Acapulco, Mexico
Construction date: 1998
Photographs: Alberto Moreno

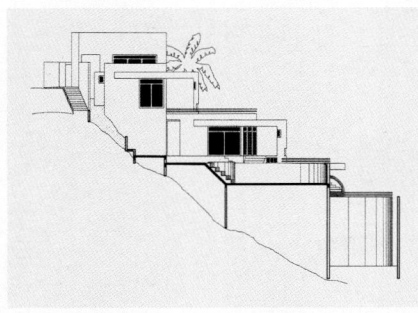

The Villa Nautilus, located in the city of Acapulco, was conditioned by the project site and those aspects of the program that most interested Migdal Arquitectos: topography, climate, function, views, and tectonic character, among others.

The site's extremely sharp slope assigned the project the task of acting as a cohesive element. To this end, the existing topography was reinterpreted through the construction of a series of volumes that adapt to the terrain. The morphology of the site conditioned the position of these volumes, which together form a coherent, terraced complex. This composition is altered by the entrance hall, which consists of the only block placed perpendicularly to the slope, simulating a bridge between the street and the house.

No hierarchical order was established between the different spaces: the living areas are mixed with zones of horizontal and vertical circulation. In this rich combination of environments, the service areas occupy a predetermined position. Oriented toward the west, they obstruct and filter the sun's rays, dampen the brusque climatic changes and, above all, reduce the high temperatures that characterize these latitudes.

The house is stratified in public and private spaces, each with their respective services. The living room, kitchen and dining room on the intermediate level act as the core of the house, and their facades are entirely glazed to allow the occupants to enjoy the spectacular views. The exterior zones were also designed for the owners' enjoyment and consist of alternating paved and landscaped areas.

The different levels are slightly rotated in order to encompass the wide range of views of the splendid bay. Consequently, it is possible to appreciate the landscape in different ways depending on the level from which it is contemplated. This rotation seeks a northward-looking orientation; hence the solar protection parapets decrease in size as they gyrate.

The tectonic nature of the project is inherent to the structural concept that generated it. To solve the constructional problems posed by the building's needs, it was decided to support the different volumes with bearing walls, solid stone slabs, and stone joists and vaulting.

The details are the result of a careful study. For example, part of the exterior lighting consists of tubes placed along the socles that create the transition between interior and exterior. The cladding and carpentry provide the finishing touches to a complex that is luxurious, but never ostentatious. The house concept is based on logical, rational formula including aesthetic harmony, structural discipline, and a project design governed by coherent inner laws. Given these characteristics, one might be tempted to think that the result would be excessively rigid. Yet, the house is astonishingly rich, and Migdal Arquitectos have managed to create a varied repertoire of environments that seek the material and spiritual comfort of the occupants and provide a whole gamut of gratifying aesthetic and visual sensations.

Villa Nautilus

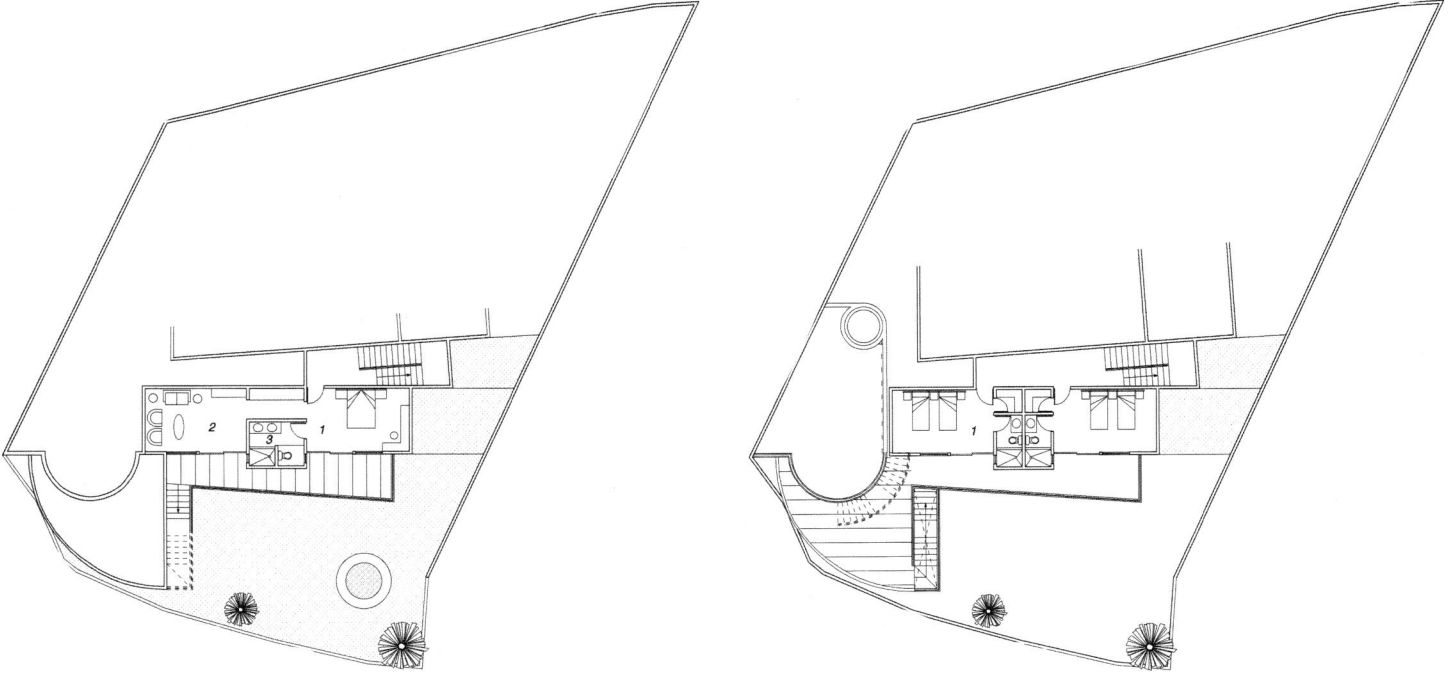

First floor.

Second floor.

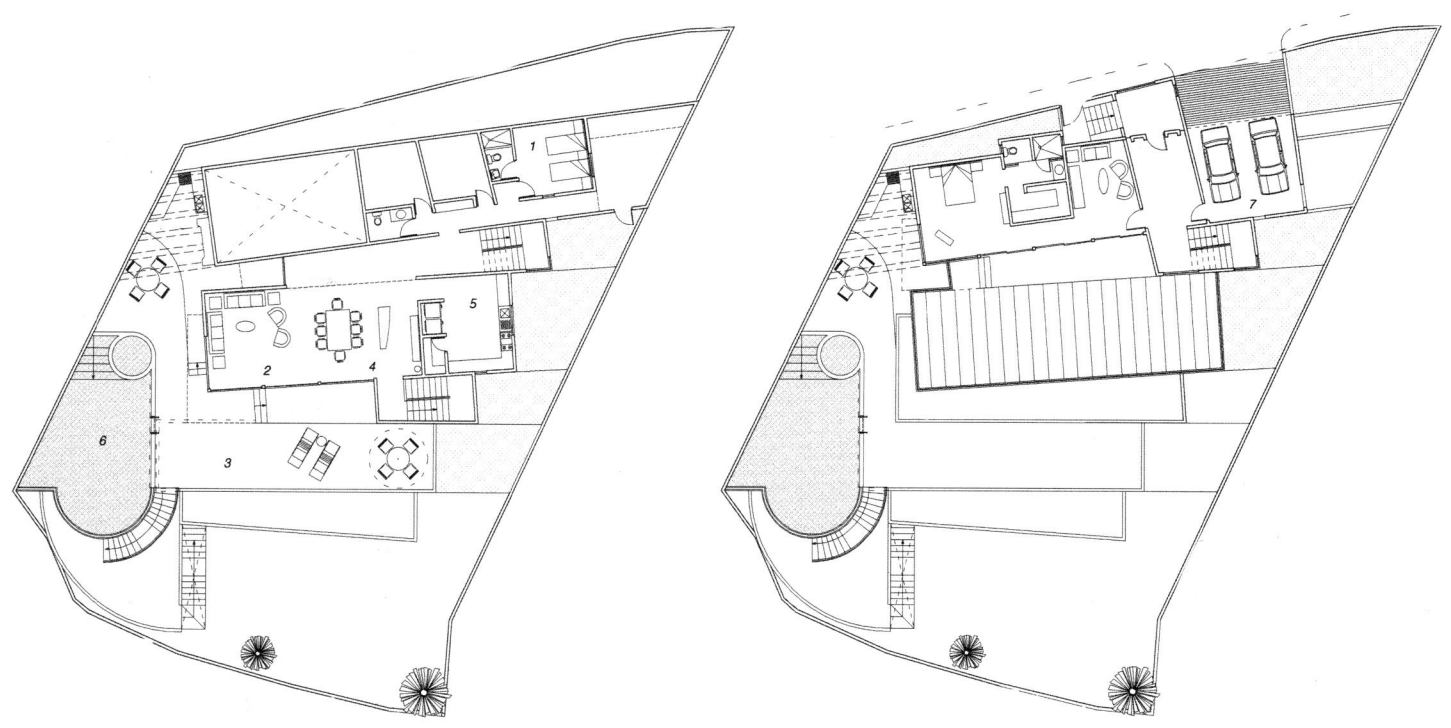

Third floor.

Fourth floor.

The house is arranged on different levels to compensate for the steep slope.

1. Bedrooms
2. Living rooms
3. Terraces
4. Dining room
5. Kitchen
6. Swimming pool
7. Garage

All levels of the house overlook the Bay of Acapulco.

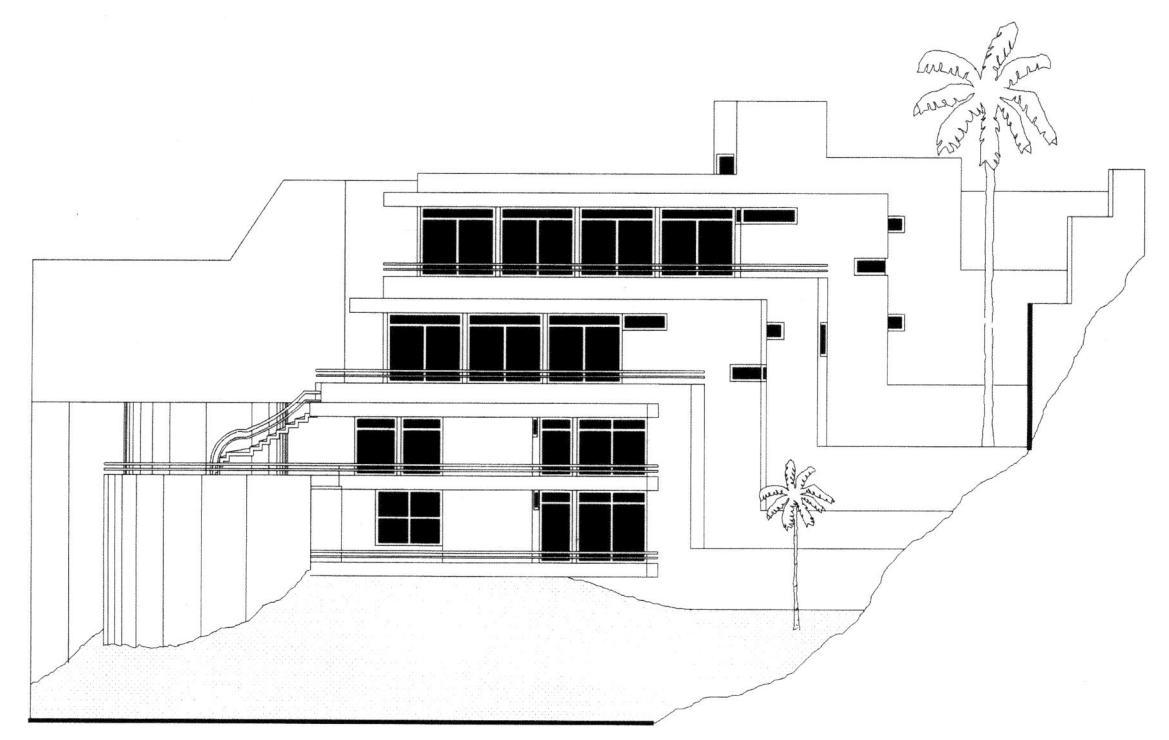
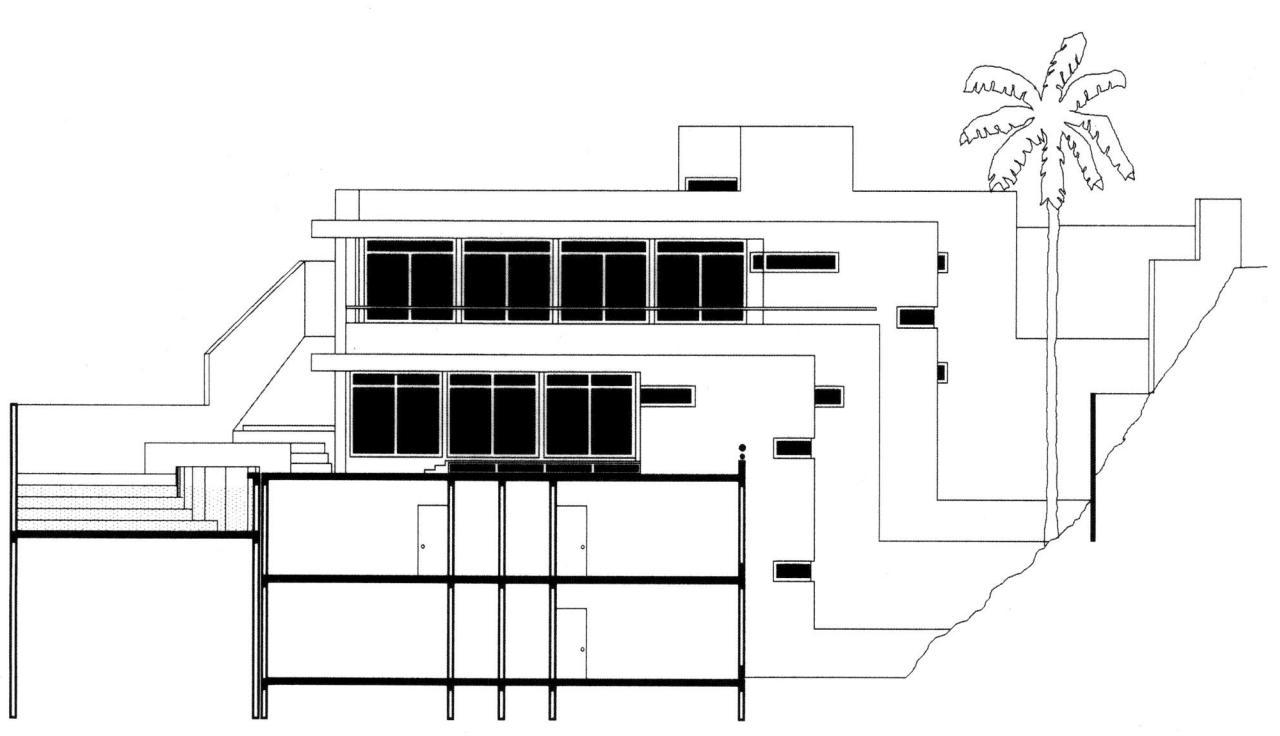

The morphology of the site conditioned the position of the different blocks, which are slightly rotated to include a wide range of views.

Villa Nautilus **47**

Architects: Döring, Dahmen and Joeressen
Location: Meerbusch, Germany
Construction date: 1998
Photographs: Manos Meisen

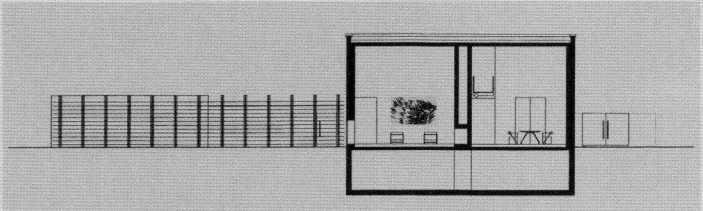

Ingenuity. Ingenuity is the basic ingredient of the Schickert House. Wolfgang Döring has responded intelligently and subtly to existing conditions and the requirements of the project. Döring surprises the observer with specific mechanisms that strengthen the virtues of the program and overcome the drawbacks of the site. At first glance, the house appears to be a typical single-family home: a conventional program contained in a simple, contemporary building set in a generous garden. However, the design details have transformed the house into a series of architectural tricks, staged in part by the delighted occupants themselves.

From the street, one can access the house by way of a rectangular patio at the north end. This first open space acts as a filter between the public space of the street and the privacy of the house. The architect offers a retreat from the bustle of city life. In order for the observer to participate in the game of sensual perception, multicolored vegetation has been planted to contrast with the white walls.

The architect paid special attention to practical aspects, and the driveway follows the side of the building up to the kitchen. From the outset, it was decided that the facade overlooking the street would be blind. The house is an inward-looking structure, since views of the surrounding urban landscape are of no particular interest.

The living and dining rooms are set in a double-height space that juts out beyond the building in the form of a metaphorical bridge between interior and exterior. This artifact, suspended in mid air, begins in the living room and ends over a small orthogonal ornamental pond, enclosed by a polished black granite wall that serves a purely aesthetic function.

This is another of Döring's astonishing mechanisms, since it allows the reflection of the fish to be seen from the living room. The house turns its back on the surrounding city outskirts and is a private space full of aesthetic and constructional distractions that delight the occupants' eye. For example, some of the windows are placed so that, from the dining room, one sees only images of the garden. The constructional system obeys a strict organization: light, insulating blocks combine with glass and a metallic structure that supports the terrace. The design of the garden perfects this authentic marvel of light and space, envisioned as a reflection of the owners' lifestyle.

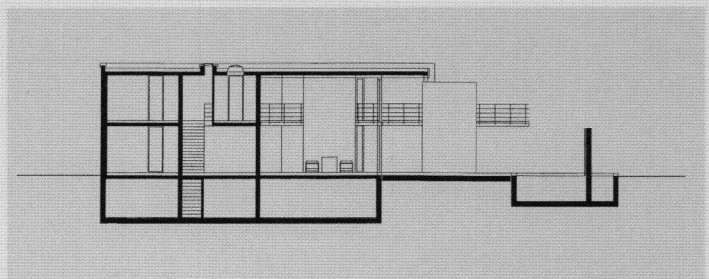

Schickert House

The house is isolated from the surrounding, peripheral urban environment and has delightful views of the private garden. Even the openings on the facade are designed to evoke images of the garden rather than of the urban surroundings.

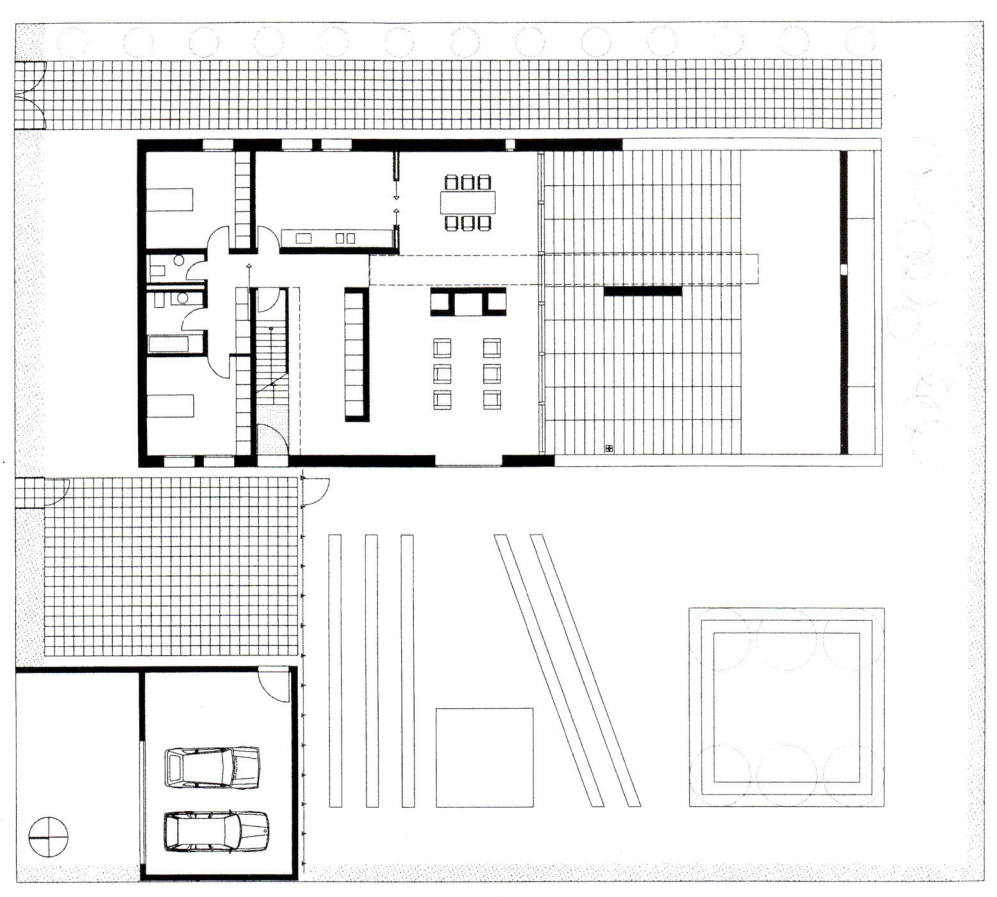

> Like a museum, the interior spaces exhibit a number of works of art on clean, elegant surfaces. Transparencies and reflections play an important role in the house's image.

Schickert House **53**

Architects: Döring, Dahmen and Joeressen
Location: Recklinghausen, Germany
Construction date: 1997
Photographs: Stefan Thurmann and Gruner & Jahr

A generous budget, ideal site and solicitous clients do not guarantee success.

While it is true that these conditions foster the design process, they may also lure the architect into the trap of excessive opulence and superficial extravagance, even leading to the materialization of his absurd delusions as creator of the world. Although these potential traps were present in the case of the Wierich House, Wolfgang Döring took skillful advantage of them to build a functional, sophisticated residence.

The house is located in the northern zone of the Ruhr and occupies a quarter of a 17,000 square-foot plot. The project is the result of clear, though flexible, ideas, and any exceptions were made to the occupants' delight. The first decision was to concentrate the functional program into a rectangular structure, whose essential orthogonal quality was broken in order to orient the living and dining rooms toward the southwest.

Structure is an essential part of the project. To compensate for the stresses produced by the sloping terrain, the main body is made of reinforced concrete. The added triangle that accommodates the living and dining rooms is made of steel, and captures natural light thanks to an entirely glazed facade.

The ground floor contains the most extensive part of a complex functional program. The staircase and elevator well separate the occupants' and service rooms from each other. This vertical connection links the different levels of the house, from the cellar and the garage to the top floor, and acts as a patio that admits light through its glazed sides.

At street level, we find the project's main attraction: a greenhouse for the cultivation and collection of orchids. Along with the swimming pool, sauna and water purifier, the greenhouse requires a zone of specific installations that is housed in the second basement.

Besides fulfilling all the functional prerequisites, the Wierich House also provides the owners with an architectural promenade on the top floor. This itinerary begins at the stairs, around which the house is articulated, and proceeds through the balcony and gallery, both with vistas toward the interior and the garden.

The exterior spaces are the brainchild of Bernhard Korte, who designed a series of metal cubicles combined with porches and orthogonal areas of greenery. The garden design provides additional exterior living areas and is another example of the care lavished on all parts of the house.

Wierich House

The entrance to the house combines the materials found in the living room and other interior spaces: concrete, glass and metal carpentry.

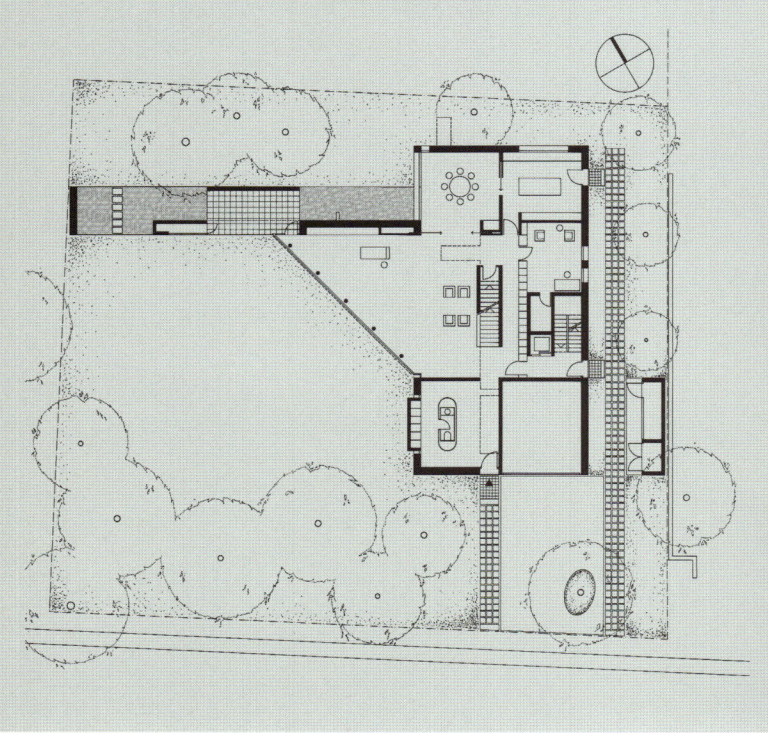

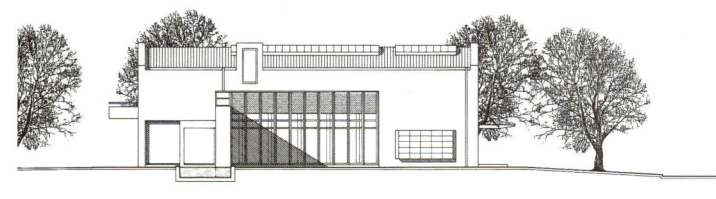
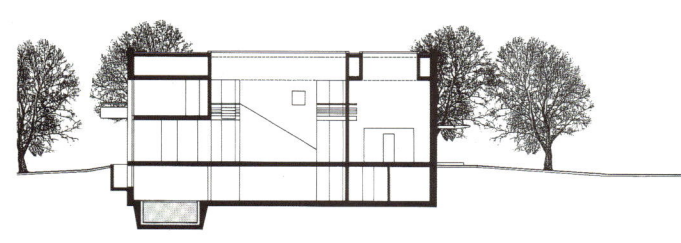
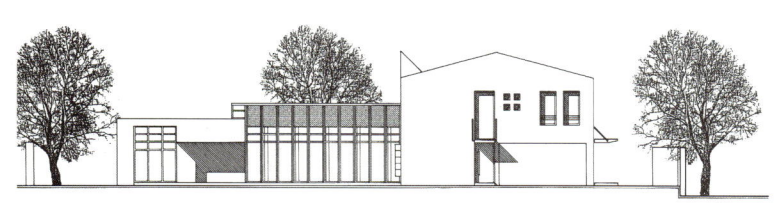

58 Wierich House

The ground floor accommodates most of the complex functional program. The staircase separates the living areas from the service rooms.

The top floor includes interior balconies from which it is possible to enjoy views of the ground floor and the garden. The stairs and corridors are upgraded as belvederes.

Architect: Dieter Thiel
Location: Schopfheim, Germany
Construction date: 1998
Photographs: Klaus Frahm

Dieter Thiel, a renowned German designer of furniture and objets d'art, has been thoroughly successful in this, his first venture into the world of architecture. He has shown that thanks to a spirit of research, it is not only possible to come up with a valid project, but to simplify it from the conceptual viewpoint. Ample proof of his achievement is the extension to this house, located on the edge of a clearing in the heart of the Black Forest.

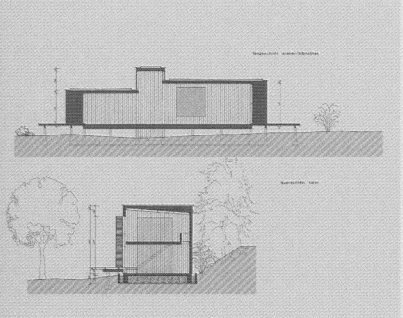

The owner, Albrecht Bangert, formerly devoted to the world of publications and art exhibitions, is now involved in advertising and multi-media. Bangert engaged Thiel to add a studio and guest wing to his house in Schopfheim, where he decided to set up his base of operations. The building that accommodates the work zone provides space for a variety of functions. To the right of the front door, we find the studio with the library on one side and a tiny kitchen and bathroom behind the bookshelf. To the left, the meeting room. This complex arrangement of spaces on the same floor resulted from the juxtaposition of three volumes, or "boxes," of different dimensions.

The platform, a framework of pillars on which the studio stands above ground, also provides a link to the guest wing. This two-story cube is positioned obliquely to the work area and contains a living room, bedroom and bathroom. The materials used in the extension are key elements that resolve not only functional but also environmental and conceptual conflicts. In the studio, the pinewood structure links the ceiling, walls and floors, and eliminates the need for pillars. The American redwood, brought especially from California, functions as exterior walls, paving and window shutters, and makes other types of cladding unnecessary.

Redwood has exceptional properties. In the first place, it does not require subsequent chemical treatment, since it is naturally resistant to woodworm and other pests. Furthermore, it is weatherproof and stands up to changes in temperature, and also has excellent static properties and a high coefficient of thermal insulation.

The structure was computer-designed by Swiss and German engineers. The sections were studied for a whole year and some of the results are truly spectacular. For example, the structure functions without guys or metal supports and covers spans of up to 32 feet. Once it had been decided how to distribute the 65 tons of wood, assembly was completed in less than a month.

Special attention was paid to the entry of natural light. Both ends of the study are completely open and elsewhere, there is only the occasional strategically placed opening. In the pavilion, the flat roof is a huge skylight. The combination of prime elements — light, material and space — gives this first architectural project by Dieter Thiel a deceptively simple appearance, concealing experimentation, risk and stringency. An almost miraculous mixture.

Bangert House

The Bangert House stands among fruit trees and was envisioned as a piece of furniture in the landscape. The project involved the extension of an existing house to accommodate a studio and guest rooms.

The main material used was untreated redwood with no artificial textures added. The interior contains choice design furniture.

Architects: Legorreta arquitectos
Location: Napa Valley, California, U.S.A.
Construction date: 1999
Photographs: Lourdes Legorreta

With the Cabernet House, Ricardo Legorreta was once again offered the opportunity to show that intervention in an exceptional landscape does not necessarily mean its degradation. The resulting splendid house, which stands on top of a pretty hill in Santa Helena, among woods and vineyards, is further evidence of the wisdom acquired by this architect during his long career as a builder of dreams. The house has been integrated into the landscape thanks to the division of the program into a series of pavilions carefully placed on the existing topography. Owing to this operation, the opportunities to obtain views - both of the surrounding woods and the site itself - were increased.

The character of the spaces that connect the four pavilions was carefully studied, so that apart from fulfilling their individual functions, they are also of interest themselves. The living room and master bedroom are linked by a gallery that overlooks the terrace and swimming pool. Passage from one guest room to the next is by way of a path of curved walls that follow the visitor's movements. Walls play a fundamental role in Legorreta's architecture, and the Cabernet House is further evidence. On the other hand, walls act as elements that link the interior and exterior of the house. This is the case, for example, of the aforementioned curved wall that, having completed its exterior itinerary, penetrates the house and eventually defines the kitchen space. On the other hand, light passes through the substance of the walls to reach both the interior and the walls themselves, creating corners of great beauty and serenity by means of natural light.

The high quality of the spaces is the result of the search for elements that allow the owners' dream to come true: to find enjoyment and happiness in the house. The dimensions of the rooms are generous and calibrated down to the last detail, so that a sense of proportion prevails throughout. Furthermore, openness to the finest possible views does not detract in any way from privacy

The facades are composed mostly from the interior, framing the best panoramas. The predominant color was chosen for its similarity to the local red earth, and the house was called Cabernet as an allusion to the kind of grape cultivated on the property. Inside, red shares prominence with shades of orange and ocher.

Most of the ideal furniture for the house was found in Mexico and shipped directly to California. Wood prevails in both the furniture and carpentry, bringing warmth to a house clearly conceived on a human scale.

With this project, Legorreta stimulates the visitors to perceive the house through their emotions. The Cabernet House achieves one of the basic objectives of architecture: to attain the happiness of those who occupy it.

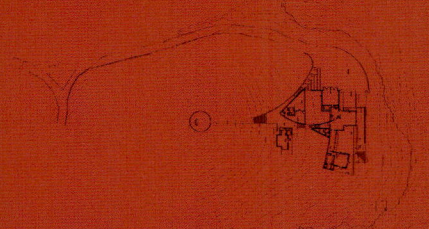

Cabernet House

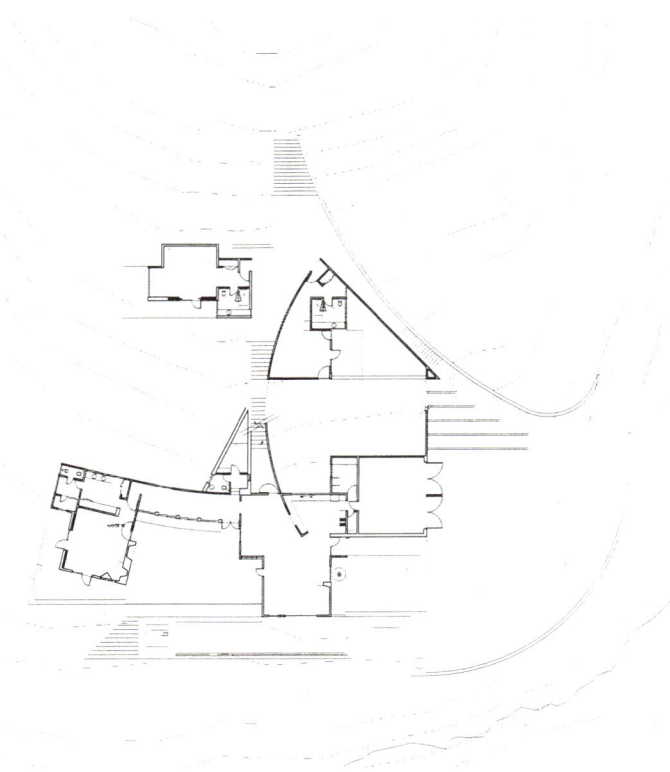

The house responds to a simple program: living rooms, master bedroom, a terrace and swimming pool, and two guest rooms. The main challenge was to establish a harmonious relationship between privacy and the surrounding woodlands.

66 Cabernet House

The sloping site made it necessary to terrace the house. Thus, it is divided into four volumes linked by spaces in between. Curved walls define the boundaries and merge with the topography, creating a sculptural complex.

68 Cabernet House

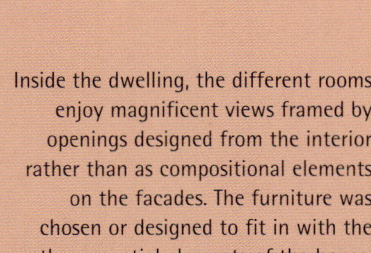

Inside the dwelling, the different rooms enjoy magnificent views framed by openings designed from the interior rather than as compositional elements on the facades. The furniture was chosen or designed to fit in with the other essential elements of the house.

Architects: Vincent James Associates.
Location: Minneapolis, Minnesota, U.S.A.
Construction date: 1998
Photographs: Don Wong

The pavilion is a recurrent concept in architectural terminology, although it rarely materializes as a physical entity. It is one of the most complicated genres because its success depends on transparency.

Architects often succumb to the sentimental idea of the pavilion — an isolated, temporary construction that is permeable to perception and itineraries. Existing reference points are the magnificent examples by Mies van der Rohe and Philip Johnson. A further paradigm of the genre is the Dayton House. Located on the outskirts of Minneapolis, this detached house in a sculpture garden is a combination of solid and empty volumes. The rigidity of the building disappears when the glazed partitions slide into the solid walls, allowing the breezes from the nearby lake to waft through the house. The most brilliant aspect of the project is its apparent simplicity.

James asymmetrically divided the site, with raised land to the northeast, and the driveway and terraces to the southwest. The built section acts as a containing wall that accommodates the garage and the service spaces. The wing perpendicular to the wall contains the dining and living rooms on the ground floor and the bedrooms on the floor above.

The enclosing walls around the site are relatively low to allow the neighbors to see both the lake and the sculpture garden. A visual passage dissects the access patio and cuts a two-story hollow out from the building, from the entry to the garden overlooking the lake. In this project, the walls are a major autonomous element. They accommodate structure, installations, the chimney and sliding doors. Furthermore, they allow smooth passage from one public space to another, eliminating the need for corridors. The structural pillars contained in these walls support a pre-stressed concrete ceiling that functions in turn as a platform for the lightweight second floor.

The Dayton House is the product of teamwork. Apart from the architects, the landscape gardener Georges Hargreaves planned the exterior spaces and the artist James Carpenter supervised the glazing.

Despite the functional requirements (the most important of which was to insulate the house from the cold winter), the design delights the occupants with its multiple views. Hargreaves sculpted the site so that snow remains to the north of the house when it has already melted to the south. The landscape also visually embraces the lake, as if it were part of the property, a luxury that not even the fortunate owners could afford.

The originality of this disciplined, multi-purpose house — pavilion, art gallery, belvedere — lies in the fact that it resolves a complex program and limited site, and enjoys relaxing views in the house and garden. Architectural stringency does not detract from the lightness of the construction.

Dayton House

72 Dayton House

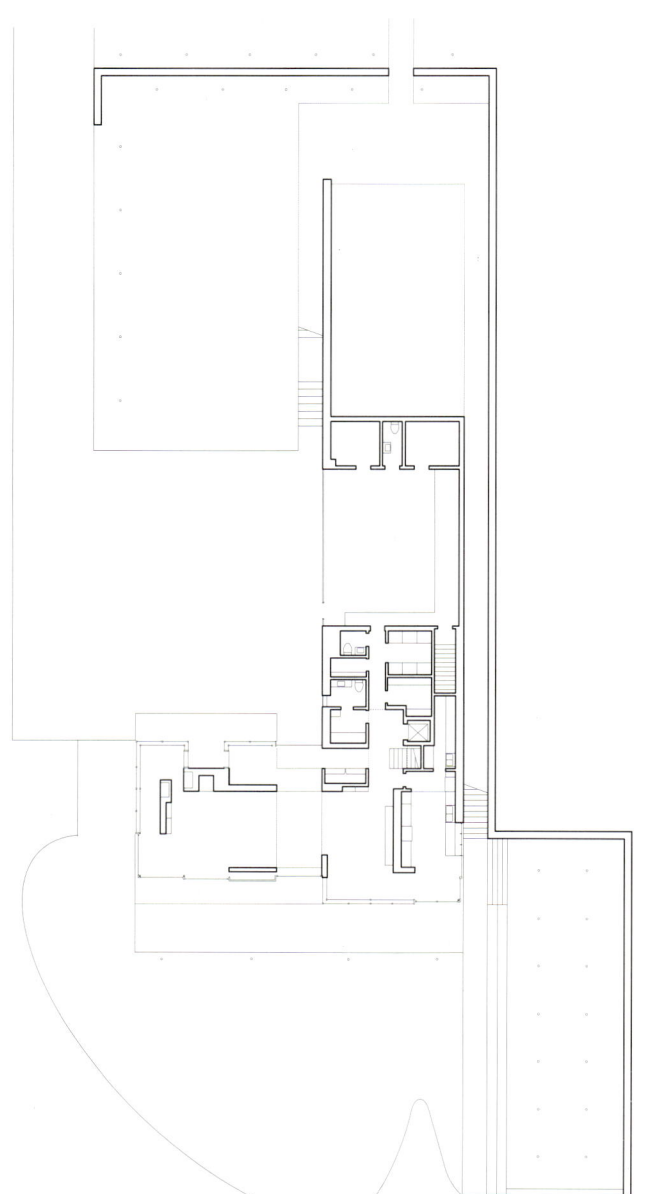
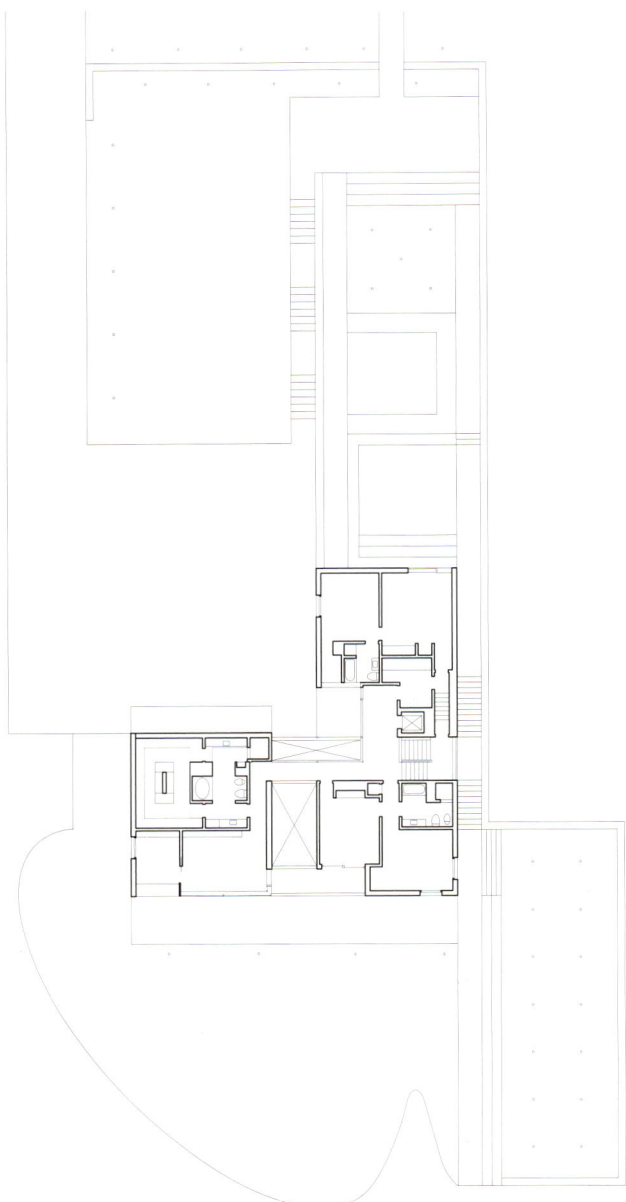

The long, L-shaped ground plan acts as a containing wall and accommodates the garage and services. The wing perpendicular to the wall houses the dining room on the ground floor and the bedrooms on the floor above.

74 Dayton House

The garden is the brainchild of landscape gardener Georges Hargreaves. Unlike his earlier works, the Dayton House project is more architectural, the result of design rather than intellectual reflection.

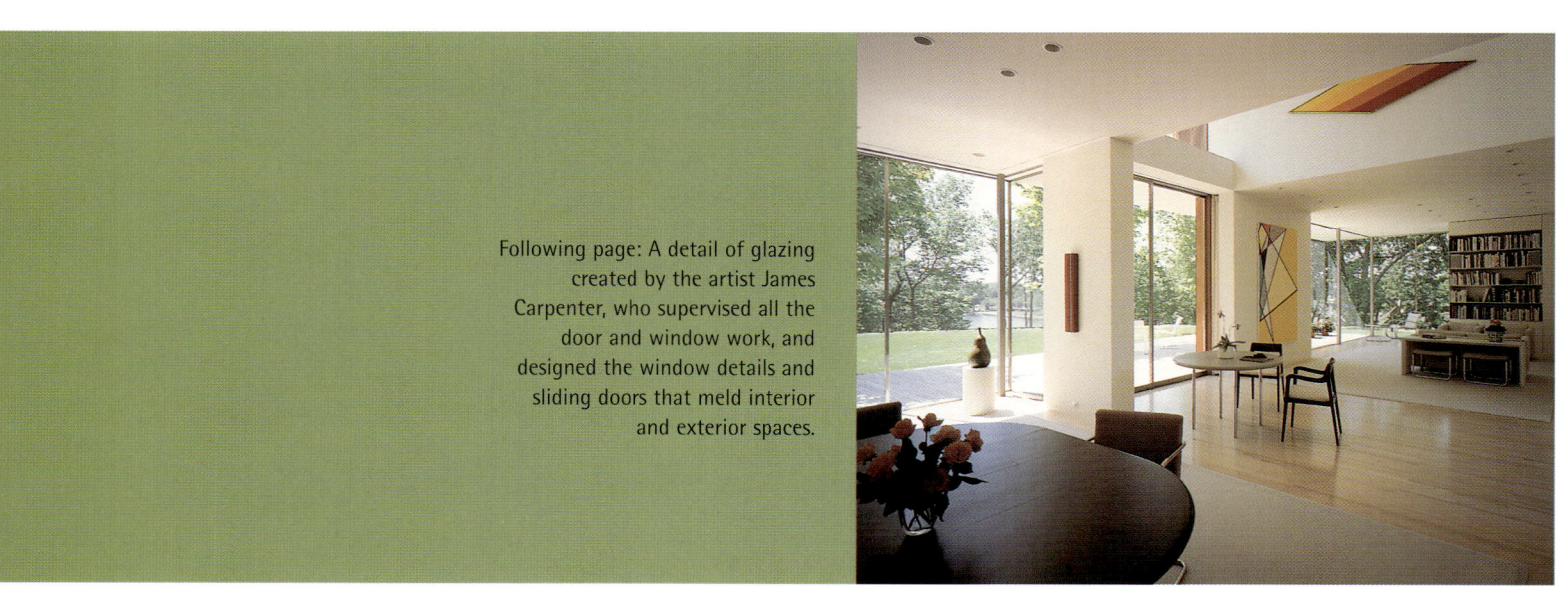

Following page: A detail of glazing created by the artist James Carpenter, who supervised all the door and window work, and designed the window details and sliding doors that meld interior and exterior spaces.

76 Dayton House

Dayton house 77

Architect: Dirk Jan Postel
Location: Almelo, The Netherlands
Construction date: 1997
Photographs: Jordi Miralles

This is a typical example that reflects the current situation in architecture and the changes that are taking place in the profession. Two aspects that differ from the traditional view of the architect's task are the client-architect relationship and control of all the building processes.

This project is based on the repetition of a module, which corresponds in size to a single bedroom and determines the structure and distribution of the rooms and the compositional rhythm of the voids. The austere container presides over the exterior and accommodates with ease what is essentially a conventional program.

On the side, facades made of sheets of serigraphed glass overlook the street and act as a kind of exterior ventilated surface. They cover the whole volume and conceal the size and position of the openings. Only the garage door and a small porch at the entrance interrupt the continuity of the cladding to indicate the point of entry. During the day, the glazed surfaces reflect the surrounding environment like a mirror; at night, the interior lighting reveals what is happening inside.

This box, which seems silent and cold from the street, opens onto the garden. Here, large French windows also obey the principals of the structural module and provide a flowing link between interior and exterior. A glass urn of exquisite purity (who would dare cover it with curtains?) acts as a winter terrace and as a symbol of the meeting of opposites. The rest of the facade is faced with light timber slats that ventilate and contribute to the friendliest side of the house, a warmth that continues inside with the birchwood paneling.

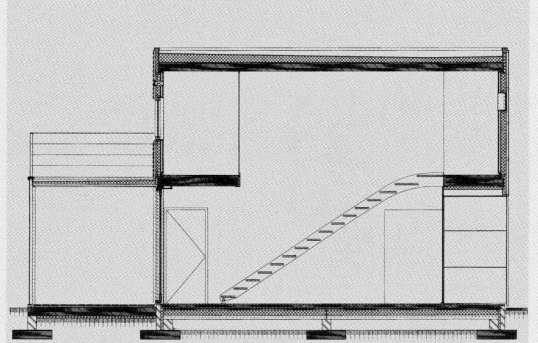

Refined construction, strict modulation and a hint of nouveau-minimalism complete the image of this small building. Undoubtedly something of a manifesto, it reflects the determination to develop the entire concept of a house, to make the minimum possible number of decisions while defending the independence of the site.

On the other hand, the way the project developed is further evidence of the rapid changes taking place in the architectural profession. The client, owner of a firm specializing in glass for construction, knew exactly what he wanted from the outset, in terms of both the program and the dimensions of each space. After the first sketches had been executed and in order to save expenditure, the plans were drawn up in reduced format and sent by fax.

The Glass House is a shining example of how to maximize productivity with minimal effort by concentrating on the clear, essential decisions needed to produce a building that is cold and refined on the outside, but warm and comfortable on the inside.

Glass House

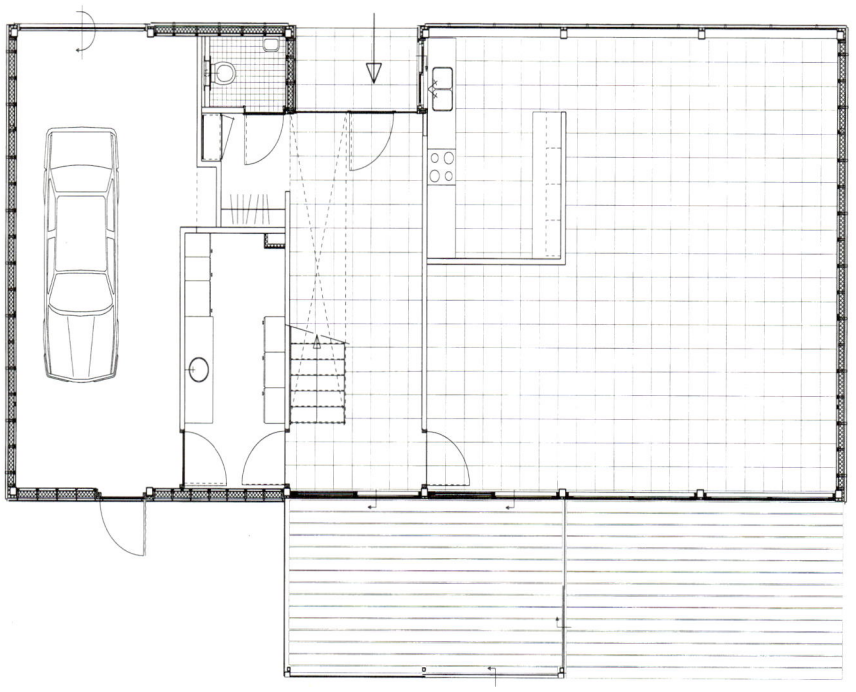

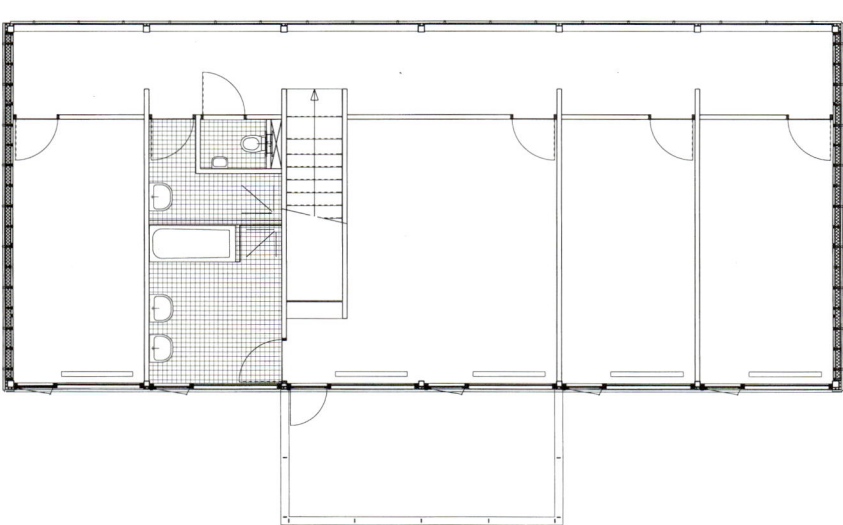

The building was based on a module corresponding in size to a single bedroom. This module determines the structure, space distribution and compositional rhythm of all the openings on the facade.

Although when seen from the street, the house appears silent and cold, it opens onto the garden by means of large French windows that are governed by the modular structure and establish flowing links between the interior and the exterior.

A minimum number of materials were used both inside and out. In contrast with the outer cladding of glass, all the interior partitions are made of wood. The doors in the house are made of translucent glass.

Architect: Kengo Kuma
Location: Hayama, Japan
Construction date: 1998
Photographs: Mitsumasa Fujitsuka

Traditional residential models are changing due to the emergence of new technologies. Materials, building methods and, above all, the computer revolution have all contributed to a new way of understanding the home. Thanks to communication via Internet, people can now carry out their professional tasks at home. Furthermore, the concept of the family is also changing fast.

Houses at the end of the millennium must allow for great functional flexibility. The structure of the house must be based on the highest possible degree of transitoriness and accept formal or practical changes without repercussions on the essence of the project.

Kengo Kuma's building responds to these demands and accommodates an artists' training center and residence. Both functions coexist in a building of pure lines whose main ambition is to meld with the adjacent wood, not only on a formal level, but also by incorporating the most conceptual parameters of Nature.

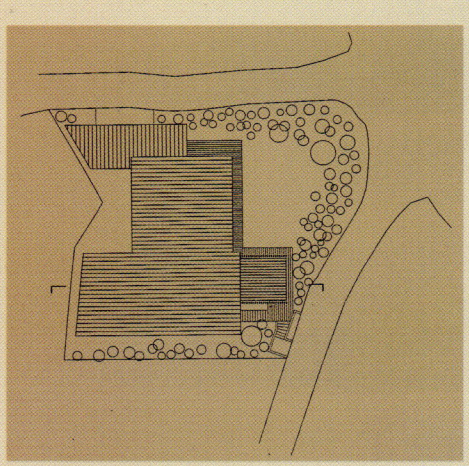

The building stands in Hayama, a city well-known as the site of the Emperor's palace and characterized as a center of cultural exchange. As in previous works, Kengo Kuma conceived the project on the basis of the least tangible architectural elements — light, water, air and landscape — thereby establishing new relationships between the resident and the object, which is no longer a fixed, rigid concept but rather an accumulation of itineraries and sensations.

The architect's main goal was to incorporate Nature and building by using vertical wooden slats found in both. The facade is made of pine slats, separated to a greater or lesser extent depending on the degree of privacy required for the room within. By means of this minimal constructional gesture, it is possible to modify the quality and function of each inner space.

Thanks to this facade, Kuma's building is perceived during the day as a neutral, impermeable volume. At night, however, the different activities taking place inside this shell can be clearly seen. From the interior, the possibility to see out depends on the distance between the slats.

Numerous environments can be created: open, luminous living areas and private, introverted bedrooms or service areas.

The ground floor accommodates the common services: the kitchen, dining room and living room, while the floor above houses the bedrooms. What distinguishes this seemingly conventional distribution is flexibility: all the different spaces share similar dimensions. Consequently, no functional reconversion would involve drastic changes to the project for the characteristic features would be maintained.

House and school

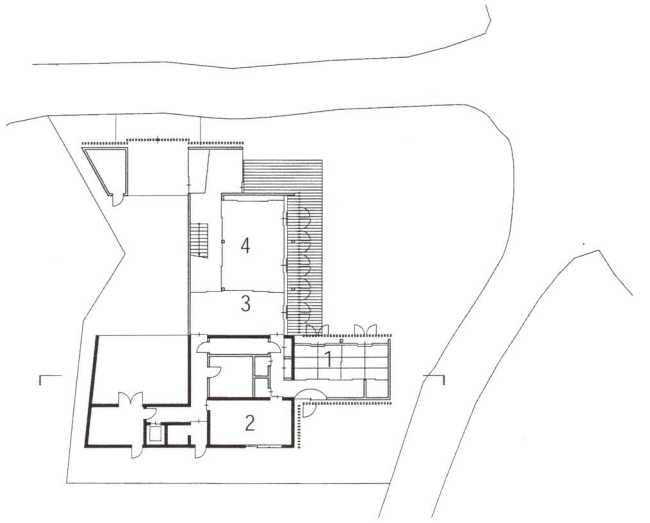
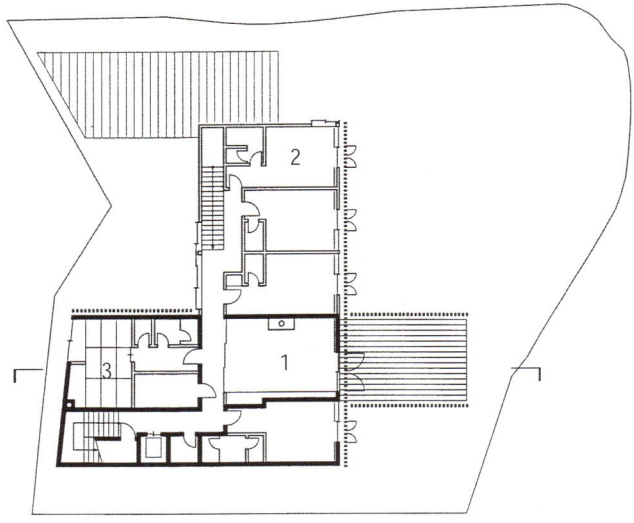

Ground floor

1. Tatami room
2. Kitchen
3. Dining room
4. Living room

Second floor

1. Living room
2. Bedrooms
3. Guest bedrooms

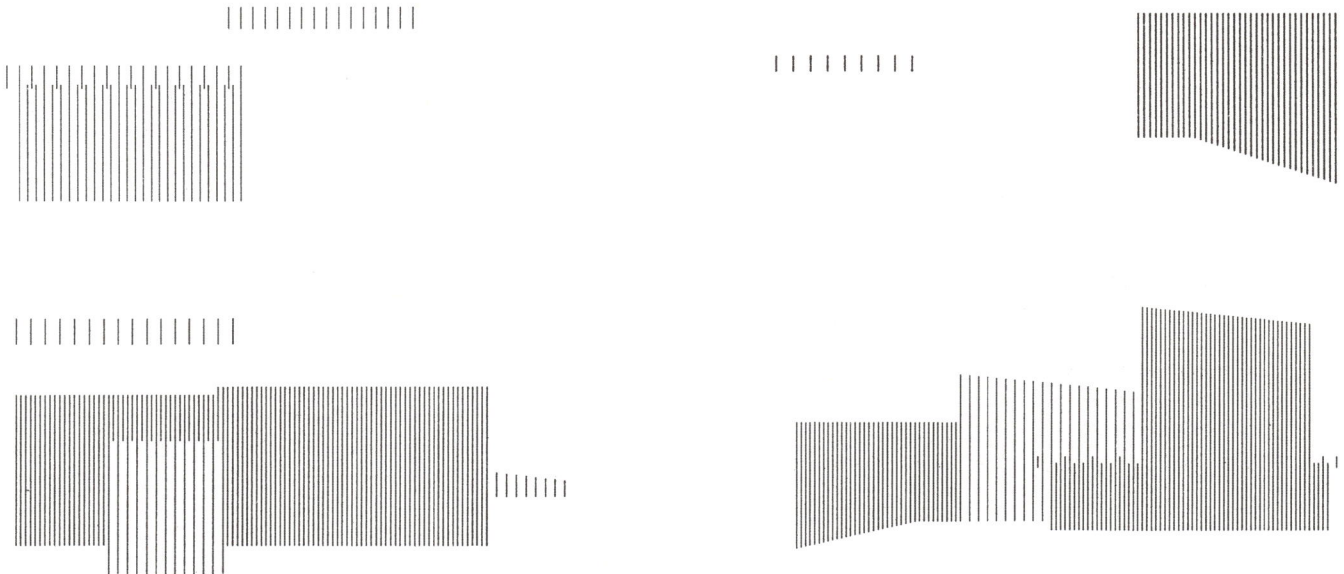

The facades are made of wooden slats. The distance between them makes it possible to regulate the light entering each room. The privacy of the rooms also depends on whether the slats are closer together or further apart.

House and school

During the day, the complex appears as a rigid volume, whereas at night, the different interior environments can be seen through the facade. The choice of the facade material was a deliberate one, since the architect sought to blend the building with the adjacent wood.

The almost minimalist interiors have been designed with great sensitivity to light and views.

Architect: Tonet Sunyer
Location: Madrid, Spain
Construction date: 1994
Photographs: Ángel Luís Baltanás

Single-family homes are the ideal framework for architects to grant themselves certain liberties in the design process. They are also one-off projects that require a substantial dose of responsibility from the architect. In the case of this building, a number of existing factors determined the final result. The Sendín House is the product of reflection on the current site, and it responds intelligently to each determining factor of the surrounding environment.

The site, some 32,400 square feet, slopes gently down to the drive. Oriented southward, it has views over the mountains of Madrid to the north. The house stands on a platform, with the parking area below at street level. The owner's brief required a single-family home and a graphic-arts studio. Therefore, the objective was to devise a project that would accommodate the different uses and an exterior landscaped garden while respecting the independence of the different components.

The living area looks southward and is protected from sunlight in the heat of summer by a large exterior porch of wooden slats. A principal requirement was that this room should be oriented in two directions so that the occupants would be able to enjoy views of the Sierra. This prerequisite became the central theme of the construction. Standing in the epicenter of the site, the living area is flanked by two wings, the first of which contains the kitchen, services and guest rooms, with their own living room and porch. The second wing contains the bedrooms and is defined by the stairs that climb up to the master bedroom and down to the office, which is linked to the rest of the studio.

The volume that encloses the south patio is two-story, although at first glance, this fact cannot be appreciated from outside. However, as visitors walk up the drive, their perception of the building transforms as they discover the elevation created by the vertical link between the basement and the ground floor.

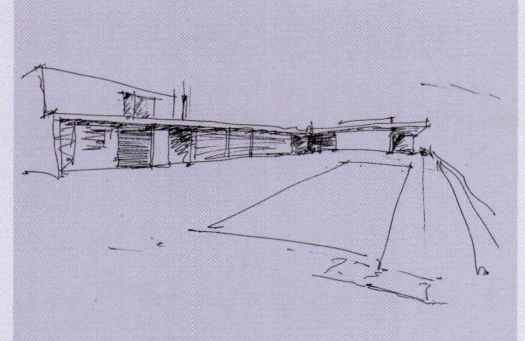

The two patios are linked around the studio. The patios provide substantial natural light and views from the basement, sidestepping the impression of being underground. In this way, the work area is never visible from the house. Similarly, those using the studio enjoy the privacy afforded by the dry gardens in the patios. The house's design places special emphasis on the exterior spaces, since they have a direct relationship with the living areas. Different kinds of landscaping separate the itineraries toward the studio and toward the house, determined by the orientation of the access to the site. The south garden acts as a filter to ensure the family's privacy and clearly indicates the different entry directions.

Once again, Tonet Sunyer surprises us with a sophisticated, elegant residence that shuns ostentation and employs the subtle interplay of natural light to enrich the different rooms of the house.

Sendín House

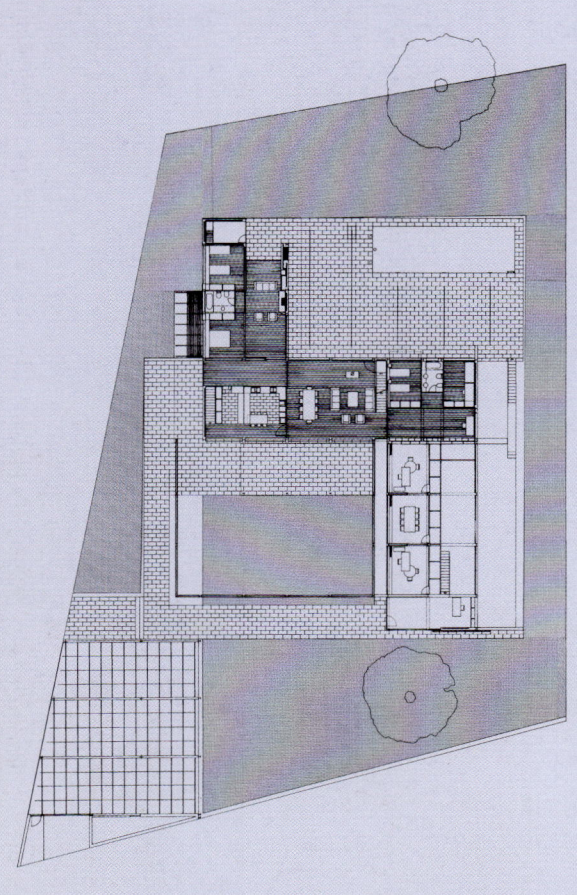
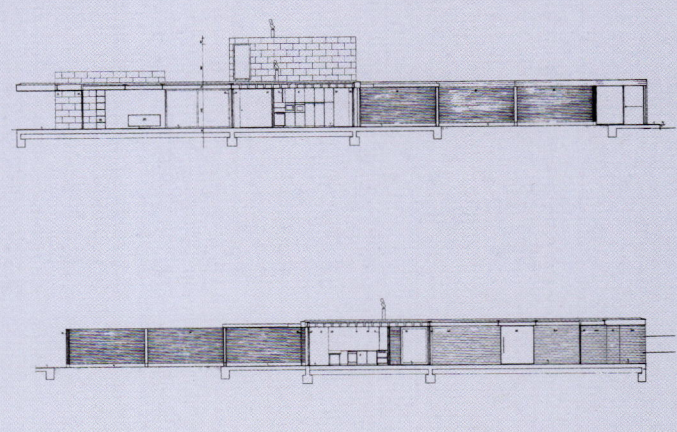

The house is the product of reflection on the site, its geographical situation and the climate. It responds to each of these factors by means of positioning criteria and the choice of suitable materials.

The central body accommodates the living area and enjoys fine views of the Sierra. The exterior metallic porch with wooden slats deflects direct sunlight.

The interior spaces are characterized by abundant natural light. The chosen materials and surface finishes enrich the house with quality and comfort.

Architects: Orefelt Associates
Location: London, United Kingdom
Construction date: 1995
Photographs: Alberto Ferrero

This residence forms part of a complex of five houses next to the legendary Portobello Road market, in what was formerly a furniture warehouse. The different buildings are arranged around a garden, and the common space also includes a parking area for residents.

After long negotiations with the local authorities, two of the five homes — this house for Gunnar Orefelt being one of them — were given planning permission as a combined home and work place.

The building is thus divided into two clearly differentiated zones: the residence and studio, each with its own independent access from the garden. The exterior appearance of both is radically different. The studio has a curved facade of zinc sheeting with circular windows, while the house is a white volume of straight lines, made of light blocks of concrete.

The house opens onto the southward-looking garden. On the ground floor, two bedrooms, a bathroom and a guest bathroom coincide with the parking lot, a storeroom, a junk room and a boiler room. The floor above contains the dining and living rooms in a single longitudinal space, with the workroom at one end and the kitchen — the only room that looks onto the Portobello street market — at the other. The studio is a double-height space linked to the house by a spiral staircase. At the top of the stairs, we reach a gallery-library before entering the dining room. When necessary, this space is used as a room for work meetings. A small inner patio facing north makes it possible to open enormous windows in the studio and link it visually with the master bedroom on the ground floor and the dining room on the floor above.

The project as a whole offers a wide variety of spaces and sensations, achieved in part thanks to the multiple mechanisms that give substance to the different parts: the creation of the inner patio, the link by means of the spiral staircase, the small terrace on the upper floor, the covered terrace, the penetration of natural zenithal light, the window over the street and so on.

Only a few materials were used for this project. Two of the most significant are the limestone on the floors of the kitchen and studio and the birch plywood paneling in the study. Gunnar Orefelt designed the tables in the living room, and the remaining furniture was designed by others, including Aero, Bruno Mattson, MDF and Conran Design.

Orefelt Associates have managed to maximize the idea of combining two different uses in the same project: the juxtaposition of work and living space. The intervention's result is excellent interaction between elements.

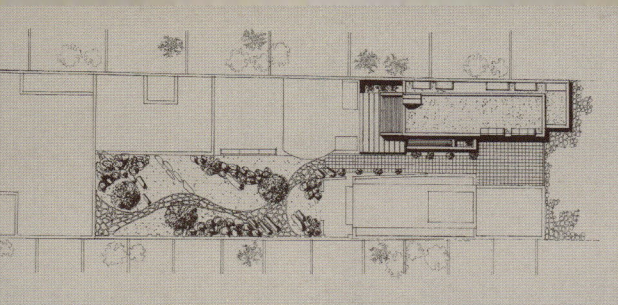

House and studio

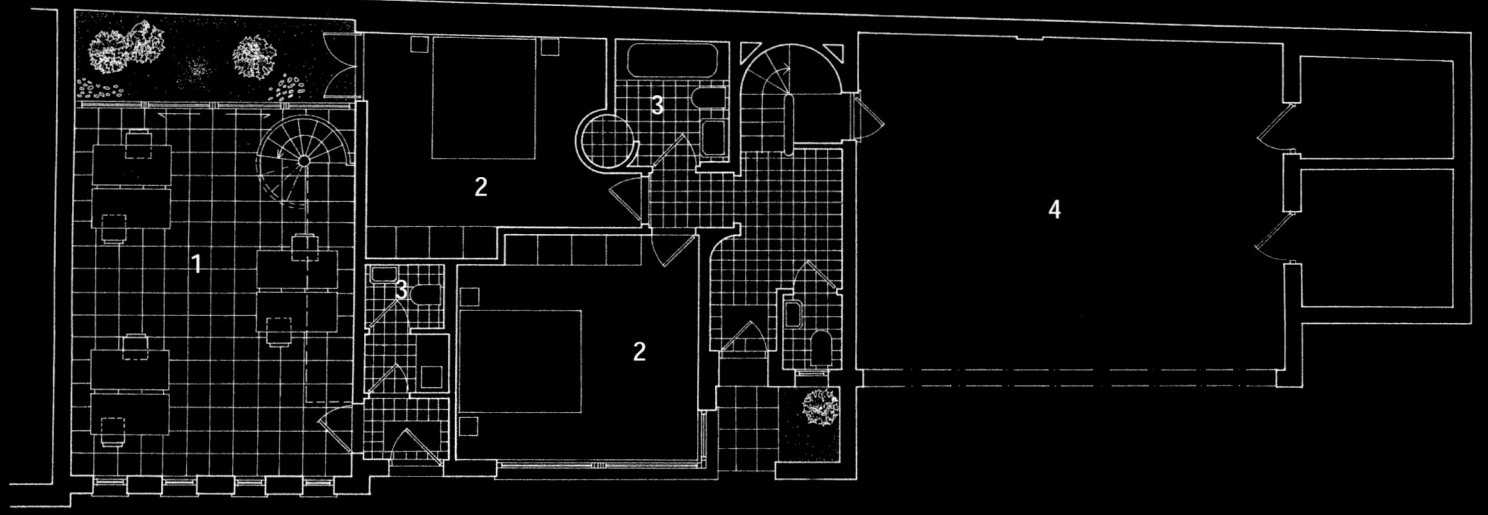

1. Studio and library
2. Bedrooms
3. Bathrooms
4. Garage
5. Void above the studio
6. Living and dining room
7. Kitchen
8. Terrace

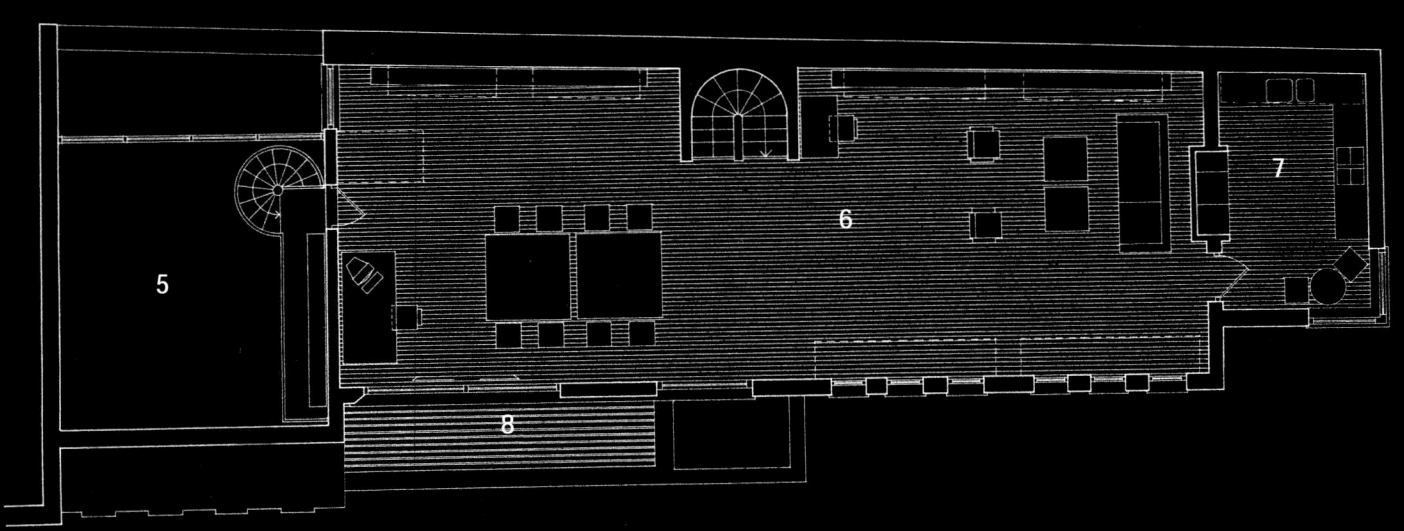

The combination of two uses in the same building characterizes this project by Gunnar Orefelt, a specialist in the restoration and remodeling of former industrial buildings. By creating a system of filled areas and voids, the project achieved the juxtaposition of environments related to each other and to the exterior.

Architects: Alberto Kalach, Daniel Álvarez, Gustavo Lipkau and Rosa López
Location: Contadero, Mexico
Construction date: 1995
Photographs: Paul Czitrom, Luis Gordoa and Marta Irene Alcántara

In a forest, we never perceive the complete form of its inhabitants. Rather, with each step, as we climb or descend, we discover a new silhouette that stands out against a background of leaves, branches and tree trunks. The essence of a walk in the woods is present in this house in Contadero, near the Mexican capital.

The nature of the site, on the southern slope of a valley, was a determining factor in the creative process. The architect Alberto Kalach was required to situate this single-family home on a sharply sloping plot densely populated with oaks and tepozanes. Kalach's strategy was to divide the plan into four habitable structures that would fit snugly into the terrain.

In order to disturb the natural environment as little as possible, these four structures on platforms follow the direction of natural routes through the forest. Three of them stand on pre-existing, vegetation-free paths that slope more gently. Another major requirement of the architectural brief was to avoid building large bearing walls that would affect the roots of trees in the immediate vicinity. Consequently, the platforms are not sunk into the ground, but rest on reinforced concrete supports that also act as tanks to catch the rainwater that falls from roofs and patios.

Concrete, steel, wood and glass are the materials that form and cover the four habitable structures. Each one has its own rhythms and proportions in accordance with its functions.

The entrance to the house is at the western end of the top structure, where a timber pergola and the urbanized space at its feet act as transitional elements from the exterior to the interior. This first structure contains the living room and dining room, oriented toward the dominant vegetation. The service center is situated behind the passageway.

The connections between volumes, levels and exterior spaces are made up of a system of stairs, ramps and bridges that link all the elements of the project and create itineraries from which to enjoy the house's unique location.

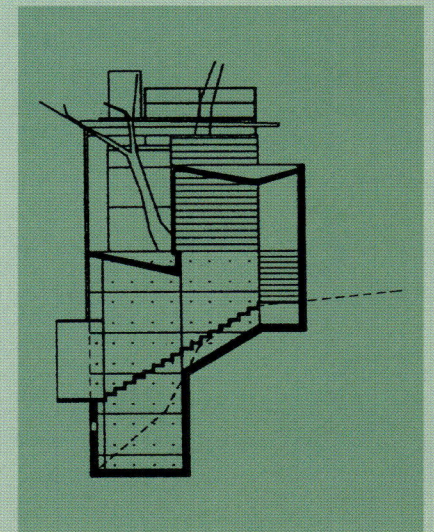

The second habitable structure contains the nucleus of bedrooms and more private areas. The bedrooms share the same orientation as the living and dining rooms, and are linked by a back passage lit from above through a skylight. A staircase climbs up from this level to the master bedroom above.

The two lower structures contain the complementary part of the house: a studio and a swimming pool, situated at the bottom end of the site. The Negro House is the sum of habitable structures of different dimensions and materials that establish a dialogue with everything around them: the mountainside, the sky and the vegetation.

Negro House

The project consists of four habitable structures in the form of large platforms that float on the terrain. Three of them stand on pre-existing paths, where the trees are less dense and the topography more gentle.

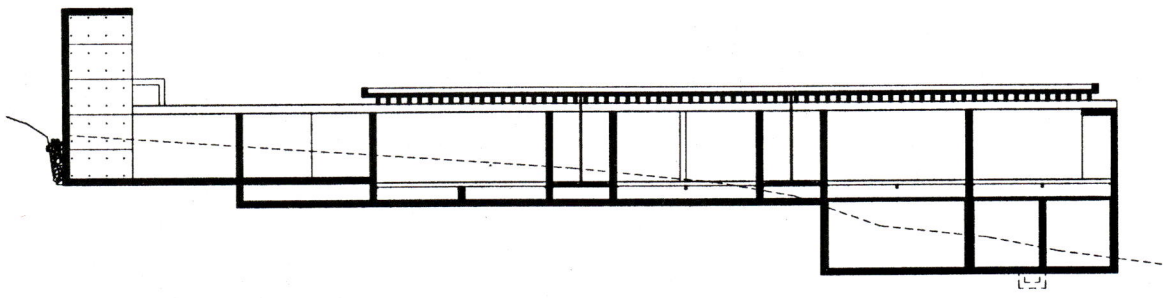

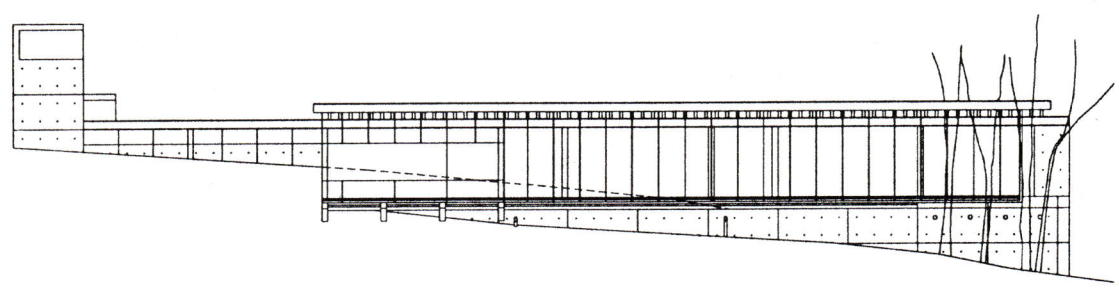

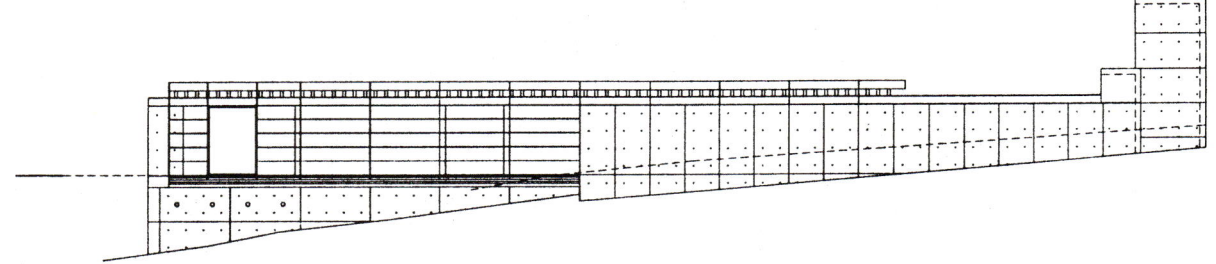

Both sections and elevations denote the architect's desire to disrupt the environment as little as possible. The platforms follow the direction of the natural lanes, and their foundations fit into the ground.

Architect: Mario Corea
Location: Teià, Spain
Construction date: 1997
Photographs: Jordi Miralles

Located near the small Mediterranean town of Premià de Dalt, the house was designed to capture the luminosity and landscape of the Catalan coast. It was conceived within the tradition of the Mediterranean house revalued as a modern solution halfway through the 20th century by Josep Lluís Sert. Mario Corea, the architect of this house, was Sert´s pupil.

Sober materials and the absence of artifacts characterize the house, designed in 1994. Light and a succession of spaces are the protagonists of a rational formula based on simple forms, predominant right angles and verticality.

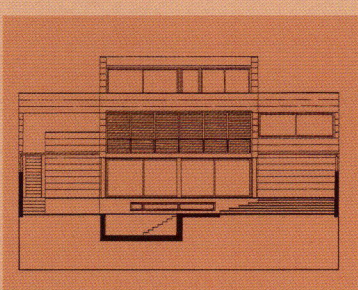

References to Mediterranean architecture stand side by side with modern materials and comfort solutions. Travertine replaced the uniform, white limestone exteriors of vernacular architecture, and in the interior of plastered walls, the traditional clay flooring has become a floating parquet of reddish wood laid throughout the house to emphasize its spatial continuity. In order for the sun to flood the whole interior, Mario Corea devised huge windows that contrast with the tiny openings in the walls of Ibizan houses. Everything here pursues vistas and sun. The desired effect is achieved, and the sea is visible from every room, including the garage, and from the swimming pool and patios on the right and left. This impression is brilliantly enhanced by the fact that the main walls and itineraries are all perpendicular to the sea, while the parallel planes are glazed to create an overall sensation of permeability and transparency. A double space between the entrance and the living area does the rest. The fireplace distinguishes the living room from the dining room, eliminating the need for interior partitions. The views in diagonal (the main attraction of the home) are embellished, and two wise decisions reinforce the attention given to different uses in the same space: the uniformity of materials is broken by the prominent use of green granite, and the hearth marks the direction of the sea and broadens the views.

The characteristic slope of the terrain made it necessary to build the house on three levels that flow into each other. This continuity is affirmed by the itineraries and empty volumes and is transmitted to the ground plan and elevations, which link the most collective area of the house to the garden, and the swimming pool to the flooring that extends from the interior to the exterior. The garden is brought into this minimalist composition thanks to the orthogonal paving superimposed on the green lawn and the blue water. The upper levels contain the rooms, designed with the same precision as the rest of the house, while the basement contains a gymnasium lit by a horizontal window beneath the porch and by an English-style patio that acts as a third, sunken garden and a new empty volume.

The house represents a juxtaposition of architectural references tempered by two clearly defined intentions: to embrace the coastal landscape and to give precedence to elegant design. The ubiquitous presence of travertine brings together references to the Mediterranean tradition, unmistakably minimalist principles and the application of interesting solutions.

House in Teià

The exterior zones have been designed down to the last detail, forming a harmonious whole. The orthogonal paving superimposed over the lawn and swimming pool brings the garden into the overall minimalist composition.

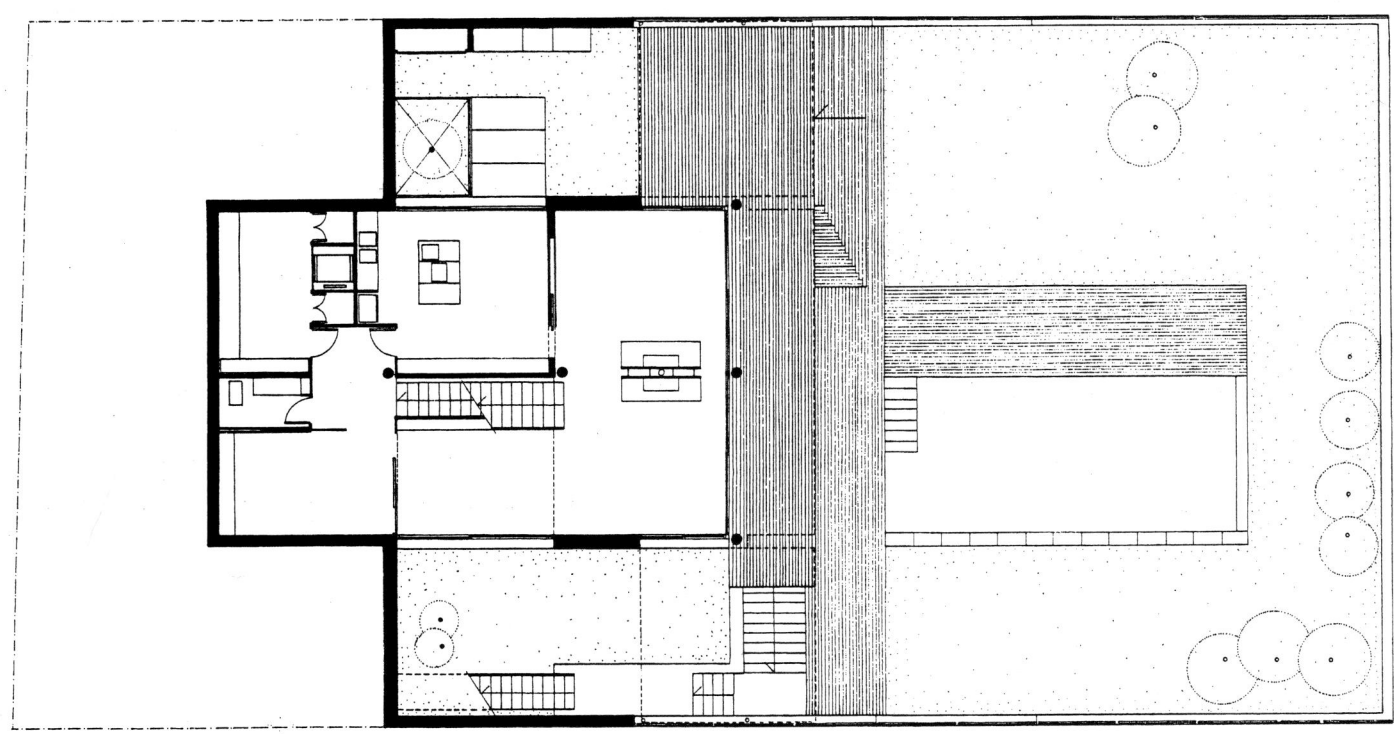
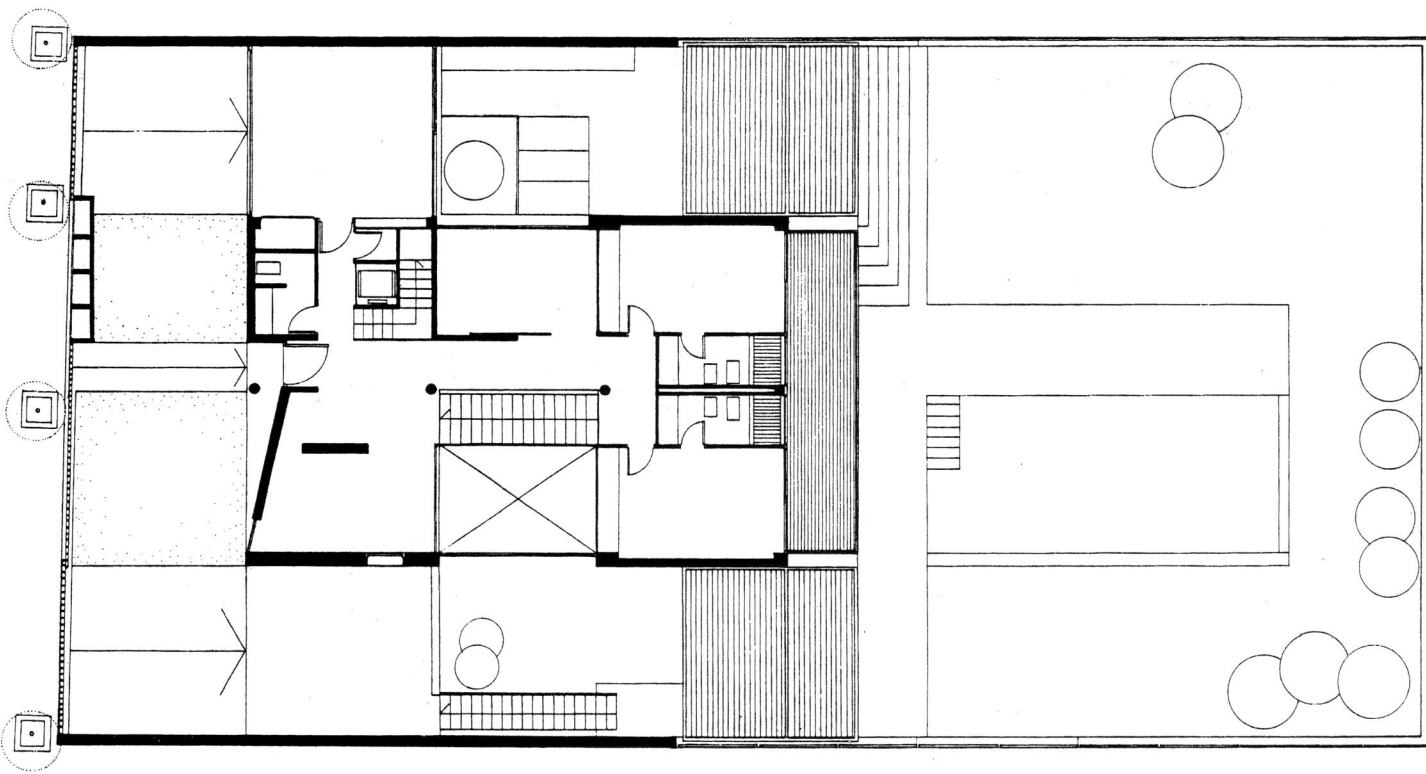

The residential program consists of living and service spaces on the ground floor and bedrooms on the floor above, which is also the entrance, since the house stands on a slope and is terraced on three levels.

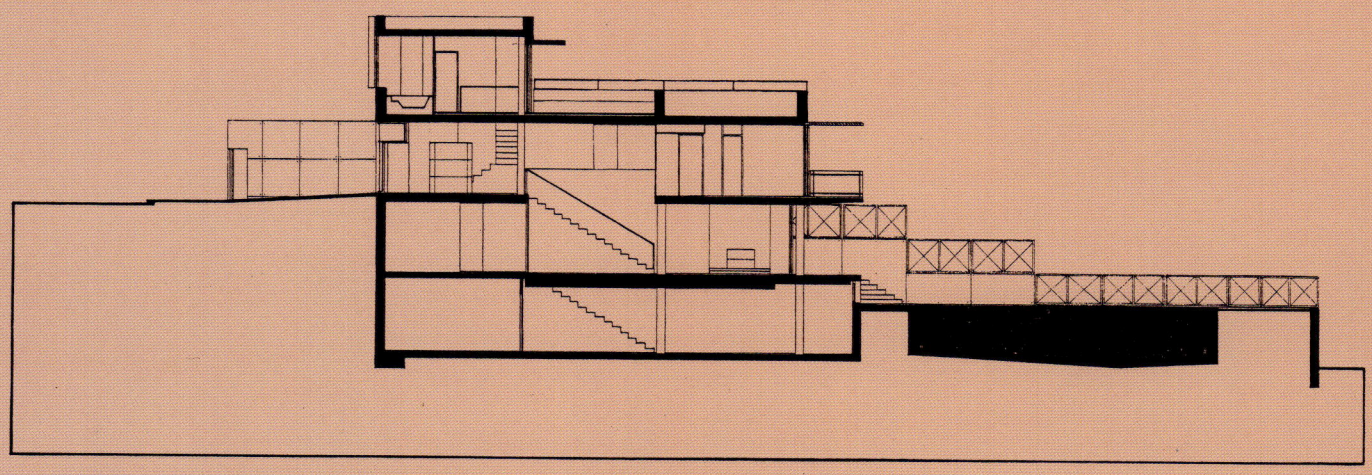

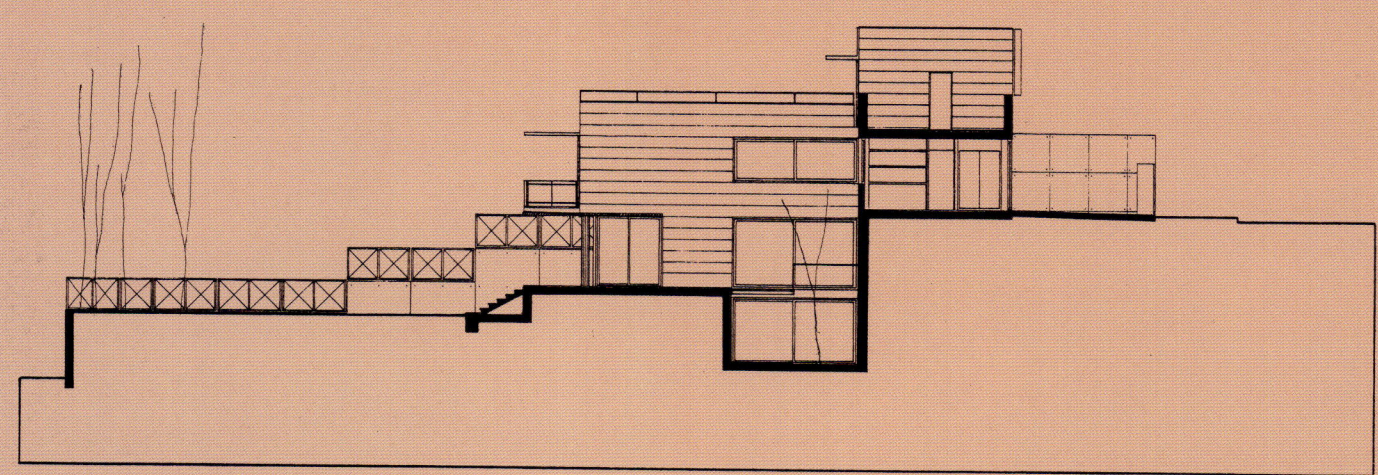

Following page

The interior spaces are governed by a minimalist principle that prevails in the use of materials and the application of simple forms. The use of travertine and reddish wood in flooring and furniture is enhanced by two dissonant elements: the fireplace and an ocher wall at the main entrance.

Architect: William P. Bruder
Location: North Sottsdale, Arizona, U.S.A.
Construction: 1997
Photographs: Bill Timmerman

William P. Bruder has once again managed to overcome the difficulties involved in harmonizing a new building with its surrounding landscape. The impressive desert that stretches before the Byrne House is one of the great assets of this project, which manages to combine large open spaces with a rich tapestry of secluded interiors.

Here, Bruder explores even further the relationship between building and landscape, establishing a parallel between the sloping concrete walls and the rocky faces of the canyons, common geological features in this area.

The house stands in the highest, northeastern sector of the site. The building's situation, together with the layout of the structural walls that are parallel to the contour lines, means that most of the rooms look toward the fine southwestern views.

The Byrne House is a split-level construction on top of the natural slope of the terrain. The entry for both people and cars is on the upper floor. The succession of walls creates lengthwise itineraries: first from the exterior to the interior and then to another open space at the far end of the house.

The hallways and corridors are adjacent to the walls, and most of the rooms overlook the desert. Such is the case on the second floor, with the kitchen, dining room, living room, large patio and a double bedroom with its own bathroom, dressing room and terrace. The floor below is also oriented southwest, although unlike the second floor, its northeastern face is underground. The main feature of the ground floor is a second living room with generous dimensions and direct access to the exterior.

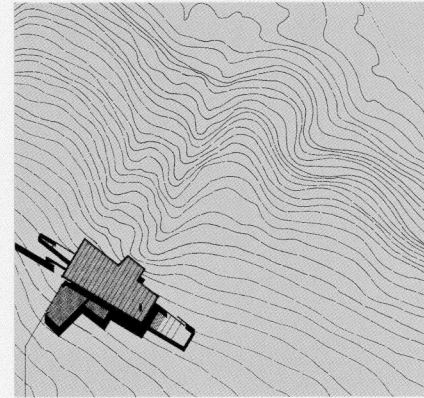

The longitudinal walls played a fundamental role in the development of the project and were carefully treated. Before the front door, they create a welcoming entrance space, while elsewhere they surround a patio. These walls establish a relationship of visual continuity between interior and exterior, and their slope frames the distant desert views as one moves through the house. Furthermore, the play of natural, horizontal light on the wall surfaces constantly changes their appearance.

In contrast to the dominant presence of the walls, the materials used for the exterior — such as copper or galvanized metal cladding — mimic the surrounding landscape. Inside the house, we find well-lit rooms with openings to suit all situations.

In short, William P. Bruder has achieved a residence in which a personal idiom of a clearly sculptural vocation adapts to and harmonizes with privileged natural surroundings.

Byrne House

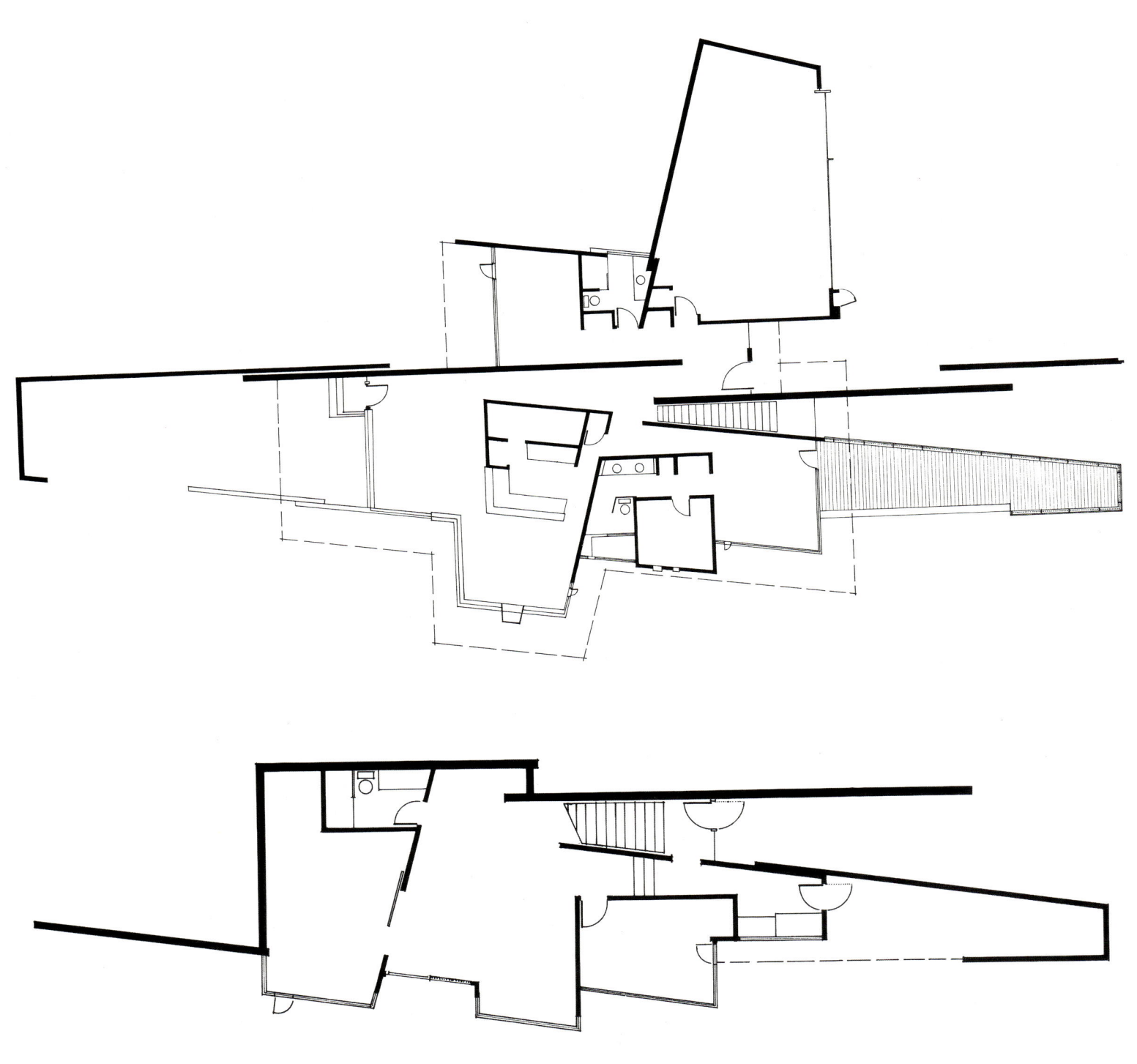

The house is inserted into the sloping terrain, and its functional program is split into two levels. Both pedestrian and vehicle access is on the upper floor, which also includes the main rooms: dining room, kitchen, living room and master bedroom.

One of the main difficulties facing the architect was to adapt his building to its surroundings, the Arizona Desert. To this end, Bruder established parallels between the construction and the rock faces of the canyons.

The house is situated at the top end of the site. Thanks to the layout of the structural walls with respect to the contours, every room enjoys splendid panoramic views.

The materials used on the exterior mimic the surrounding landscape. The copper or galvanized metal cladding harmonizes chromatically with the land.

A variety of spaces have been created inside: some extroverted, luminous and related to the exterior; others darker and more secluded, providing a greater degree of privacy.

Architect: Jordi Casadevall
Location: Valldoreix, Spain
Construction date: 1996
Photographs: Jordi Miralles

The Nirvana House is an example of successful dialogue with the surrounding landscape. Architect Jordi Casadevall has developed his initial idea in an ambitious, though balanced, way so that his project gains complexity without sacrificing clarity.

This single-family home stands on a 32,300 square-foot site in Valldoreix, a quiet residential suburb only a few miles from Barcelona.

The building stands strategically on the highest part of the site, just beside its northern boundary. In this way, part of the existing plantation of Mediterranean pines, which provides shade during the summer heat and is of considerable environmental value, has been preserved. These initial criteria provide much of the basis for the project's success, from both the conceptual and functional points of view.

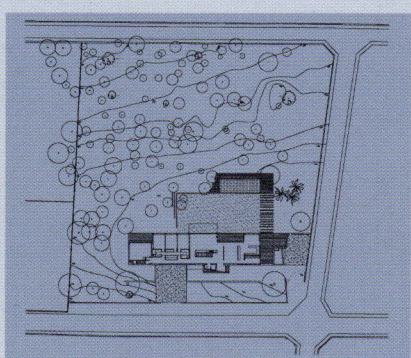

On the ground floor, the house is defined as a rigid stone-clad parallelepiped six-faced prism about 40 yards long, on which two metal cubes have been placed. The cubes house the spaces for both the owners and guests and convert the flat roof into an exterior space with its own character. The slightly disjointed position of the cubes with regard to the base and the deliberate material and color contrasts emphasize the respective properties of both elements. In this way, the solidity and rigidity of the base is offset by the two pavilions, which enrich the complex with lightness and movement.

Most of the entrances to the residence are on the ground floor, on the north side and independent from the drive. Wood is the material associated with the entrances, particularly the main one, which is the only structure added to the stone base. The numerous entrances avoid the possibility of excess circulation inside the house, and guarantee the peace, quiet and independence of the different zones.

The garage and installations are half-sunken, taking advantage of the natural slope of the terrain. A concrete wall parallel to the north facade frames the entrance to the garage and contains the different entrances into the dwelling. This simple wall is one of several simple resources used to impose a hierarchical order on the exterior space and to allow a gradual transition from the public sphere (the street) to the private one (the house).

The facades have been designed to accurately reflect what happens inside and outside the house. A number of horizontal incisions have been cut into the northern facade that gently light the lengthwise distribution itinerary while simultaneously isolating it visually from the street. However, from the southern facade, the bedrooms and living and dining areas open onto the garden and swimming pool, either directly or through porches. The transition between inside and out is so generous that on occasions it is difficult to distinguish between them.

The Nirvana House is a paradigm of how to achieve flowing interior spaces without sacrificing the autonomy of each individual part. The two interior stairs are good examples of this. The stairs are accessed almost directly from outside and link the pavilions to the rest of the house and the garage without sacrificing any degree of privacy.

Jordi Casadevall's project is irrefutable evidence of the fact that architectural stringency and skill can transform the most rudimentary plans into projects of subtle sophistication and rich complexity.

Nirvana House

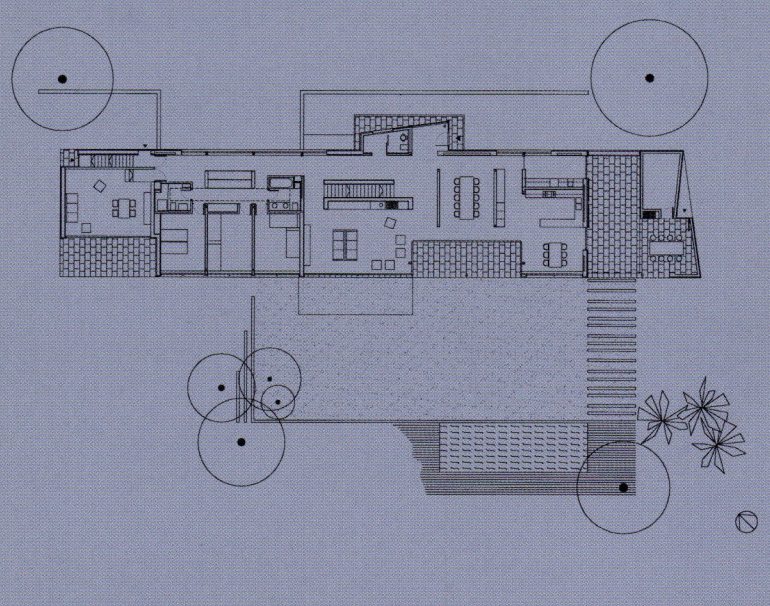

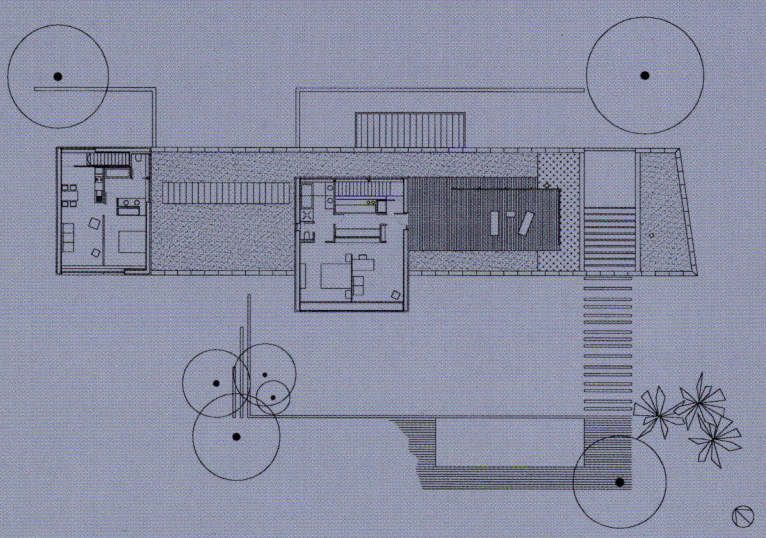

The ground floor accommodates the living and service areas. All the rooms have direct access to the exterior, which greatly enhances communications.

The floor above houses the two bedrooms, which are slightly staggered with respect to the base and thus enjoy a degree of volumetric autonomy.

The borderlines between interior and exterior are permeable, which ensures free-flowing communications and wide visual perspectives of the garden from inside.

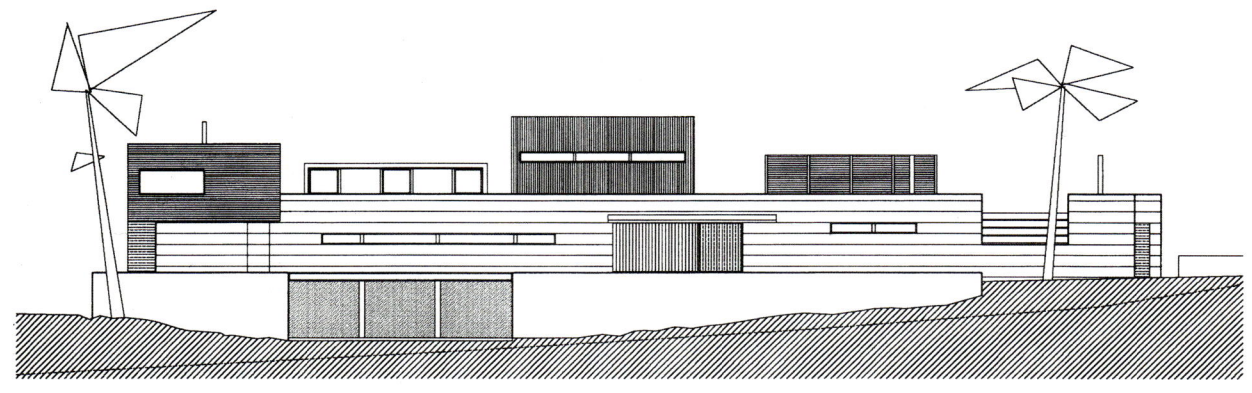
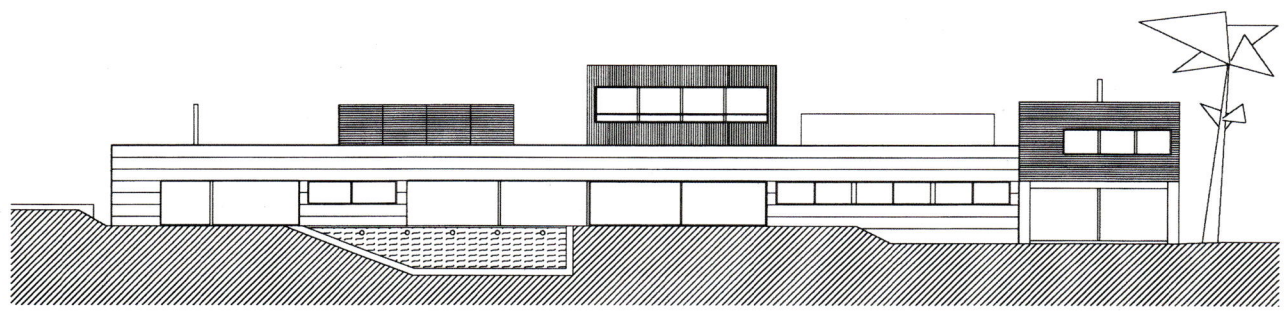
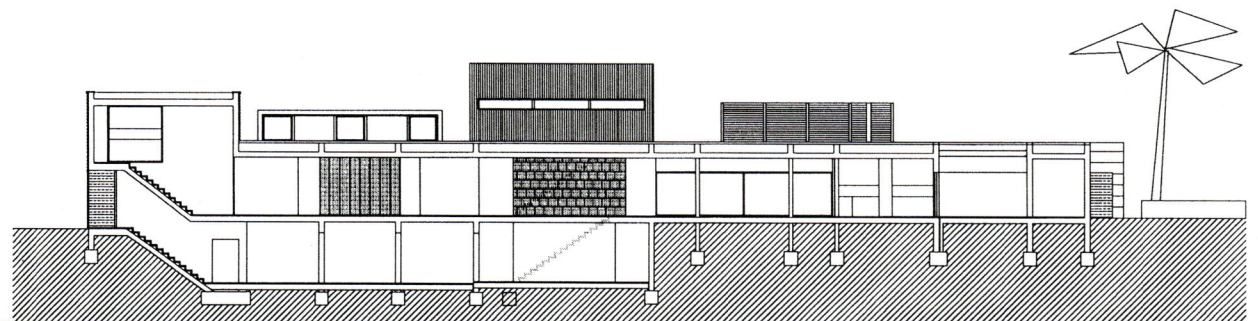

The elevations and sections accurately transmit the criteria governing the location of the house, which stands at the top end of the site beside a plantation of native pine trees.

130 Nirvana House

The two metal cubes containing the bedroom stand on the stone base of the dwelling. Their slightly disjointed position emphasizes the change of materials and use.

Architects: Baumschlager & Eberle
Location: Lochau, Austria
Construction date: 1996
Photographs: Eduard Hueber

It must be the Alpine air. There is simply no other explanation for the volume of quality architecture coming from two of Europe's smallest countries, Switzerland and Austria. Herzog & de Meuron, Gigon & Guyer, Peter Zumthor, Pauhof Architects, and others are doing fine work. Though it may be a coincidence, the fact is that an impeccable sense of rhythm and proportion and a masterful use of materials (especially wood) characterize all projects by these architects.

Heading this generation of Central European architects are the Austrians Carlo Baumschlager and Dietmar Eberle. Although they have been responsible for a wide variety of projects, they have earned the most recognition in the housing field. They design sober houses that are free of any ostentation; stylized homes with stunning views of their native region, Vorarlberg.

Their work concentrates on the process of creating the building: communication with clients in order to reach the solutions that most satisfy their needs; buildings in accord with their setting; and consideration of the different professions involved in construction. These elements combine to produce a sensitive, functional, distinguished architecture. The house in Lochau is an outstanding example of this approach. It stands on a huge site belonging to the family of the client who, with this project, ensured that no other buildings would spoil the magnificent views of the nearby lake.

The project is based on a simple idea that is both practical and striking. The ground floor contains the installations, a bathroom for guest accommodation on this level and the garage, which also acts as a multi-purpose space where domestic chores and professional tasks may be performed. The floor above houses the living area and bedrooms, while the kitchen and bathroom are located in an adjacent wing. This level is designed to be a single room, since the lack of visible physical partitions allows the spaces to flow into one another. In this way, the utility areas do not interfere with the leisure area where the best views may be enjoyed.

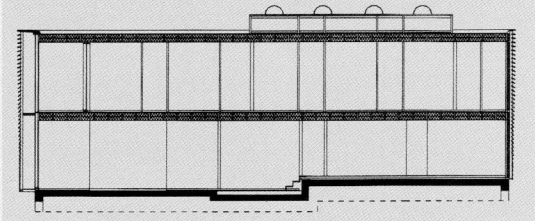

The double facade is one of the project's most interesting aspects. The idea sprung from reflection on prefabricated building elements that make construction easier and reduce costs, and from consideration of the relationship established between the building and the exterior. These principles, and the need to provide protection from direct sunlight, led to a simple, though definitive, solution: a prefabricated glass box clad in wooden slats. The distance between the slats is shorter on the ground floor, while on the floor above they are further apart and oscillate to allow the landscape and light to penetrate the interior. Baumschlager & Eberle demonstrate that a rational approach to architecture may produce coherent, flexible, elegant works.

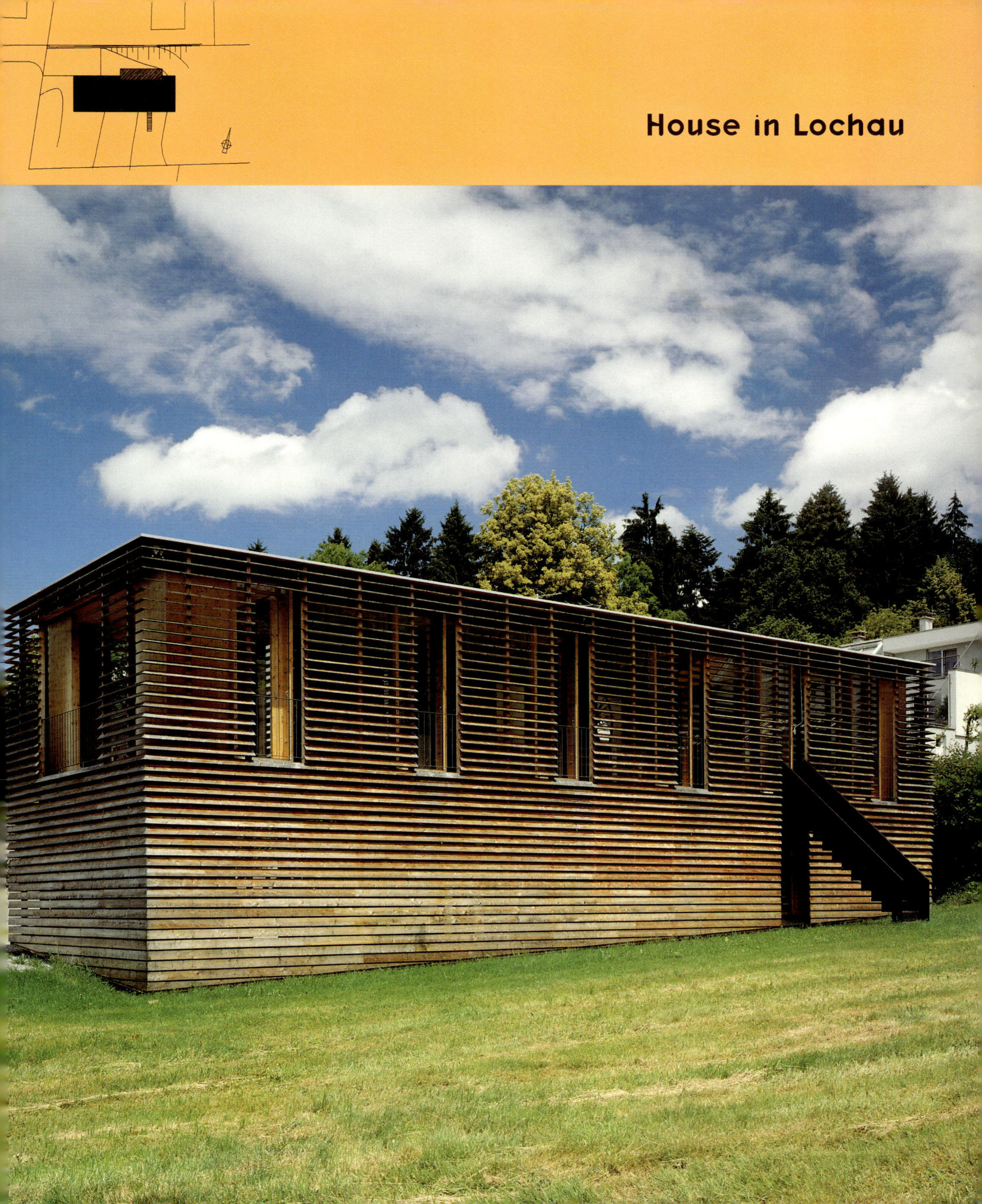

House in Lochau

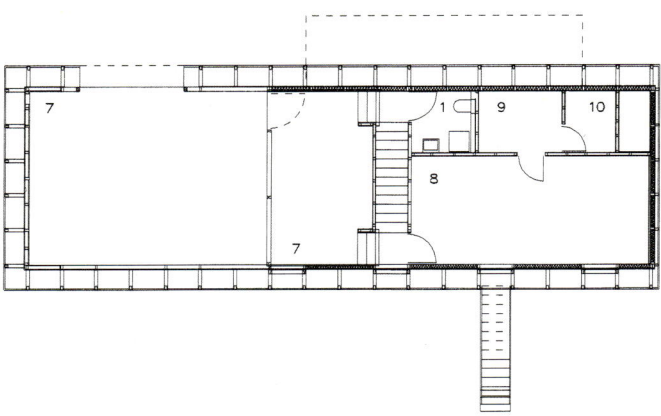

First floor.

1. Bathroom
2. Kitchen
3. Bedrooms
4. Dining room
5. Living room
6. Terrace
7. Wardrobe
8. Study
9. Installations room
10. Boiler room
11. Garage

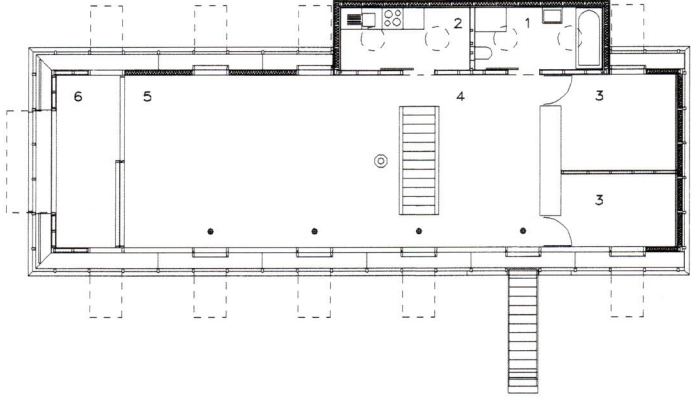

Second floor.

The architects' strategy was to reduce the project to a few definitive elements. Thus, the constructional details acquire a prominent role by virtue of the fact that they were carefully designed.

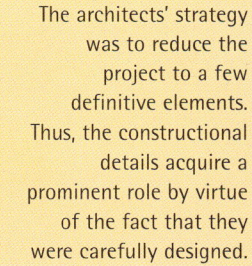

The House in Lochau was situated to take maximum advantage of the views of the nearby lake. The owners of the site guarantee that no buildings will spoil such magnificent scenery.

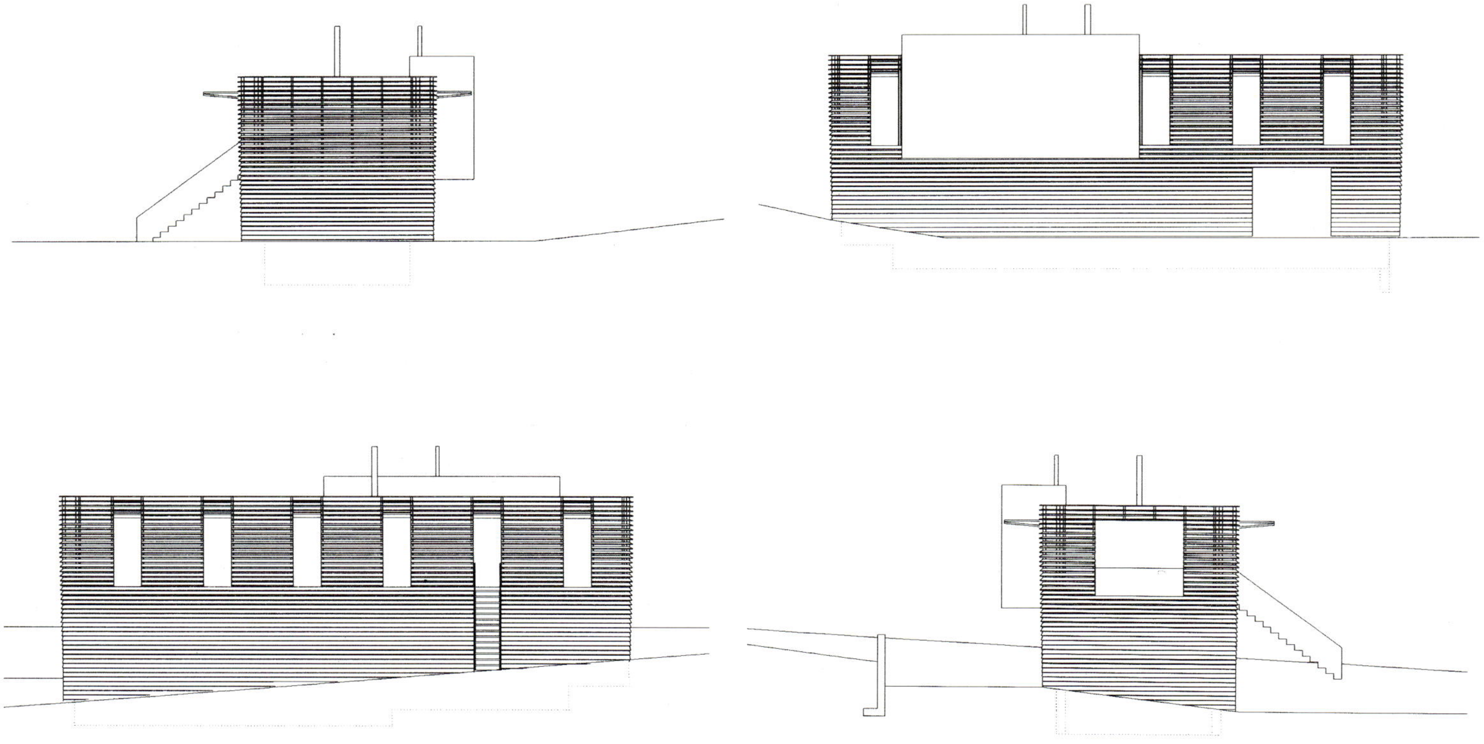

The double facade is one of the project's most interesting concepts: it consists of a glass box covered with wooden slats that regulate light penetration and safeguard inner privacy. On the floor above, the slats are placed further apart to create a flowing interior-exterior relationship.

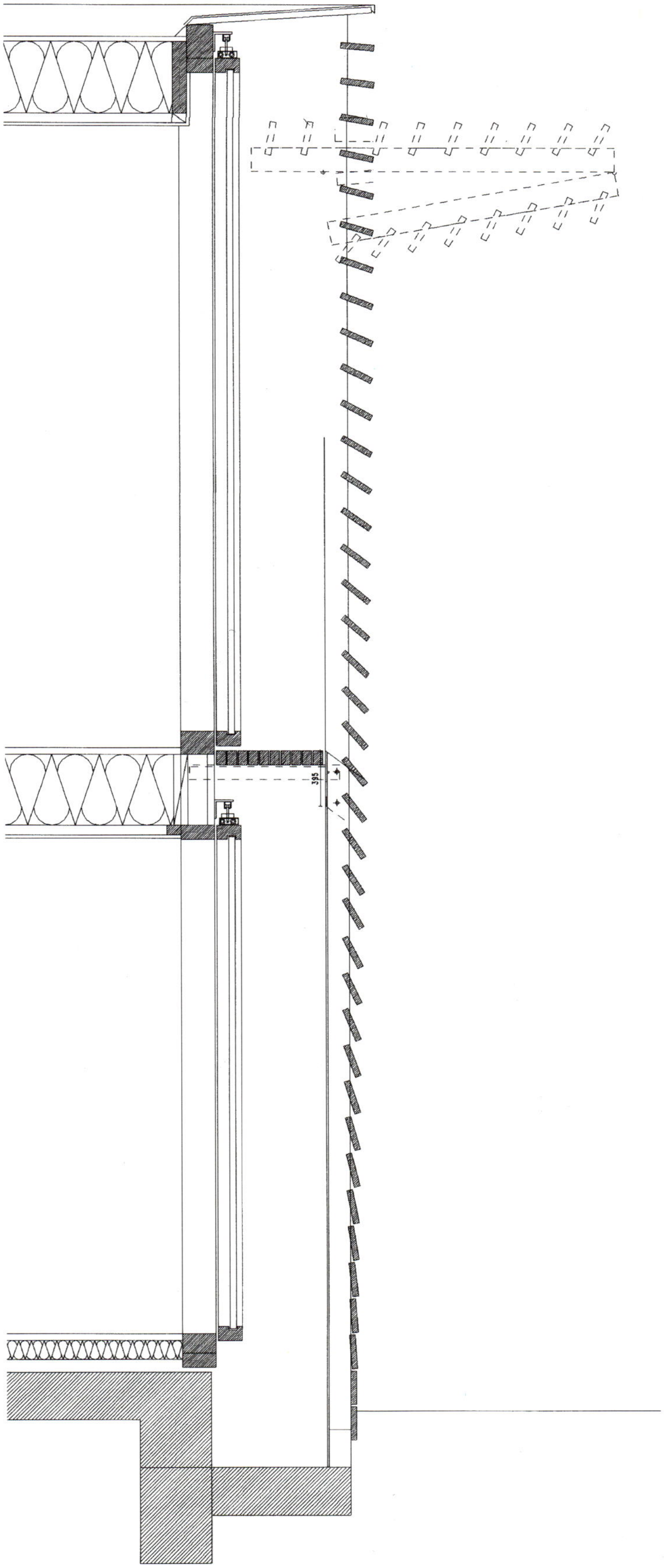

House in Lochau 139

Architects: Jubert and Santacana architects
Location: Púbol, Spain
Construction date: 1997
Photographs: Eugeni Pons, Jordi Bernadó

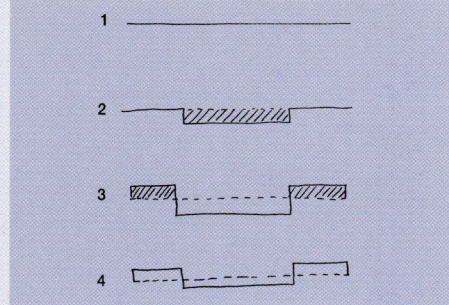

With the Jordi Cantarell House, this young team of architects has employed an effective, forceful strategy of restrained, unified building, neither excessive nor dispersed. The project demonstrates that quality architecture need not necessarily be the product of grandiose gestures.

Designed for an exceptional client — a painter and restorer of furniture —, the project is the result of a limited budget and an atypical brief: a house with reduced dimensions and a large hall in which to exhibit painted furniture. The small, gently sloping site is pleasantly orientated with fine views, and stands in a housing estate on the outskirts of Púbol, a picturesque village in the Baix Empordà region.

Two crucial factors in the definition of the building's appearance were the surroundings, of little interest, and the position of the house in relation to the urban nucleus. The intervention consisted mainly in modifying the topography and placing a section of the site on a different level from its original position.

The middle of the site was lowered to just over two feet below the access level, leaving the earth at the edges so that it would subsequently form the walls enclosing the patio. The walls acquire strength and autonomy by virtue of their role as generators of two horizontal surfaces on different levels. The first of these is an inward-looking patio sunken beneath street level; the second is a raised garden. Both surfaces are linked by an exterior stair.

By means of the earthworks and construction of the walls, the architects managed to isolate the house from its immediate surroundings without sacrificing the visual reference of the Castle of Púbol. On the walls at the northern end of the site, a volume was built that leaves a void in the basement. The space open to the exterior is the residence, which consists of two bedrooms, a living room, dining room, kitchen and bathroom. The container is the exhibition hall.

The project defines its own landscape and enhances contemplation of the patio below, which is overlooked from inside. A stair and ramp guarantee independent access to the house and the exhibition hall. Outside, to the east of the patio, a small annex was built containing a bedroom and bathroom that establishes a visual link with the house.

The north facade is sunken, while its southern counterpart, with views over the patio, takes advantage of the climatic conditions. Four glazed panels connect the living space with the exterior patio. The desire to reveal the austerity and purity of the materials governed both interior and exterior finishes. The exterior cladding is characterized by homogeneity. The galvanized metal panels and the iroko wood openings add a further touch of distinction to an already elegant facade. Jubert and Santacana have designed a multi-functional space distinguished by exquisite aesthetics and composition. Their strategy, influenced by structural logic, has accentuated the favorable qualities of the site and masterfully secluded those areas of the house most in need of intimacy.

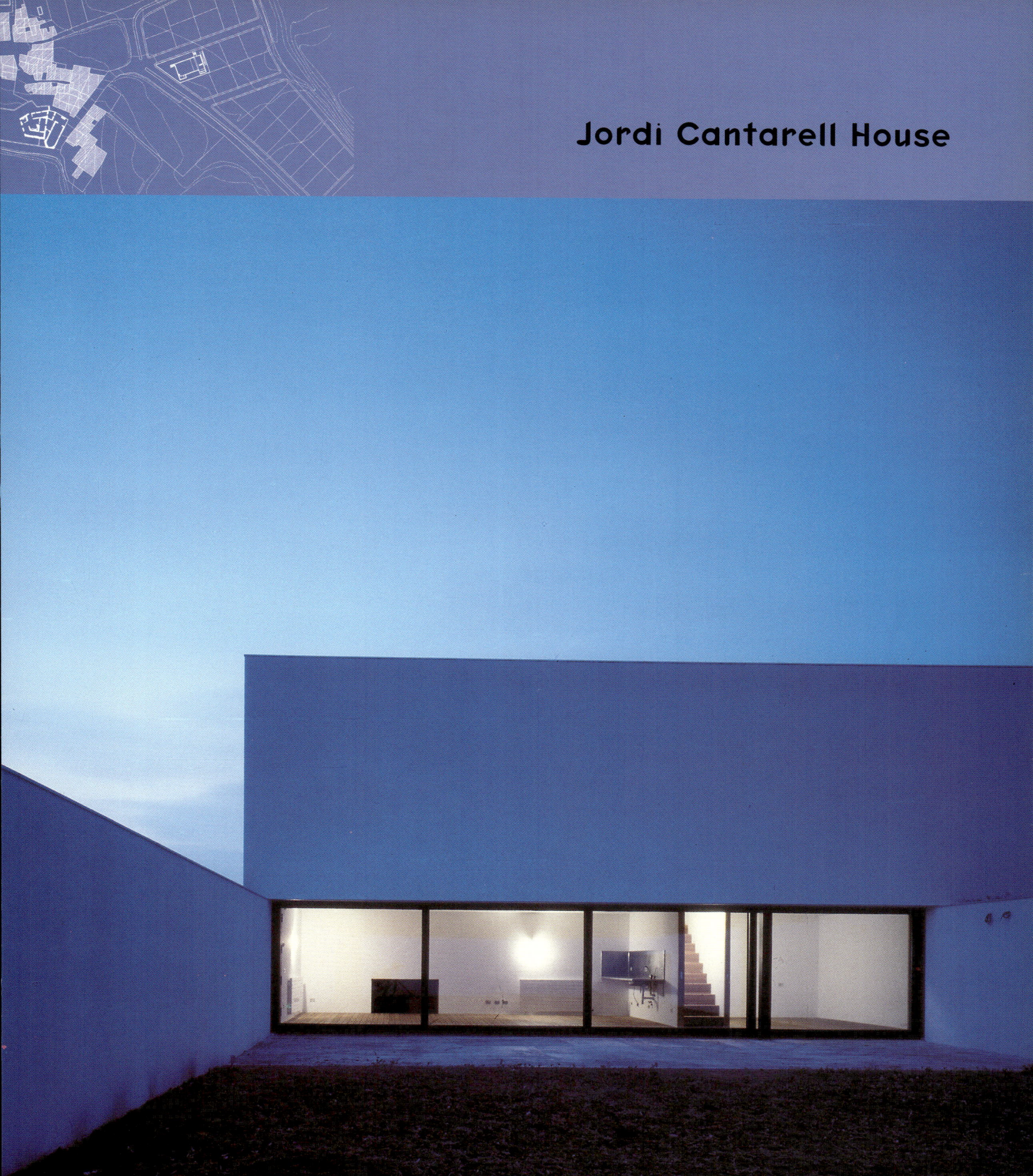

Jordi Cantarell House

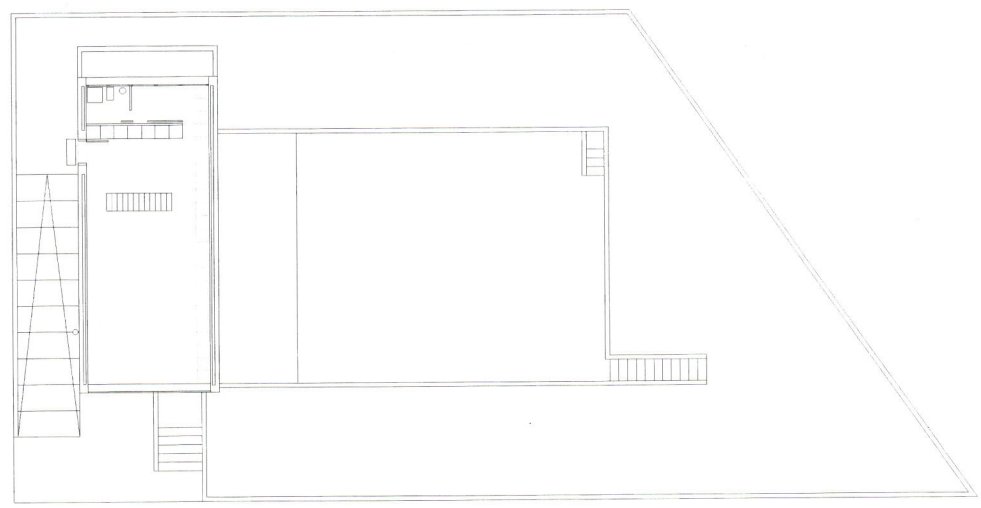

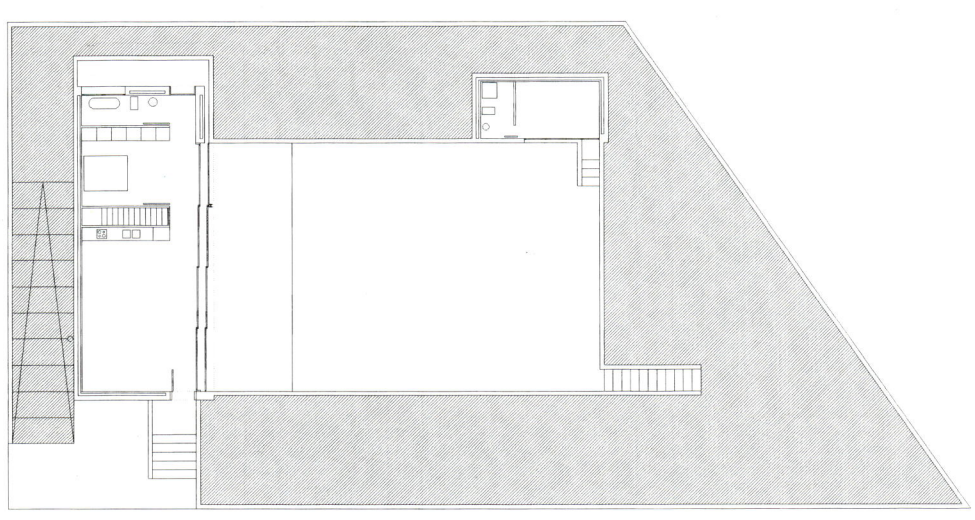

The building defines its own landscape, enhancing the views of the patio below. The Castle of Púbol acts as the focal point for views that link the house with its surroundings.

The program includes a domestic zone and an exhibition hall. The first is accommodated on the ground floor and consists of a single space containing the living room, kitchen, dining room, a bedroom and a bathroom. The exhibition hall is on the floor above.

Jordi Cantarell House

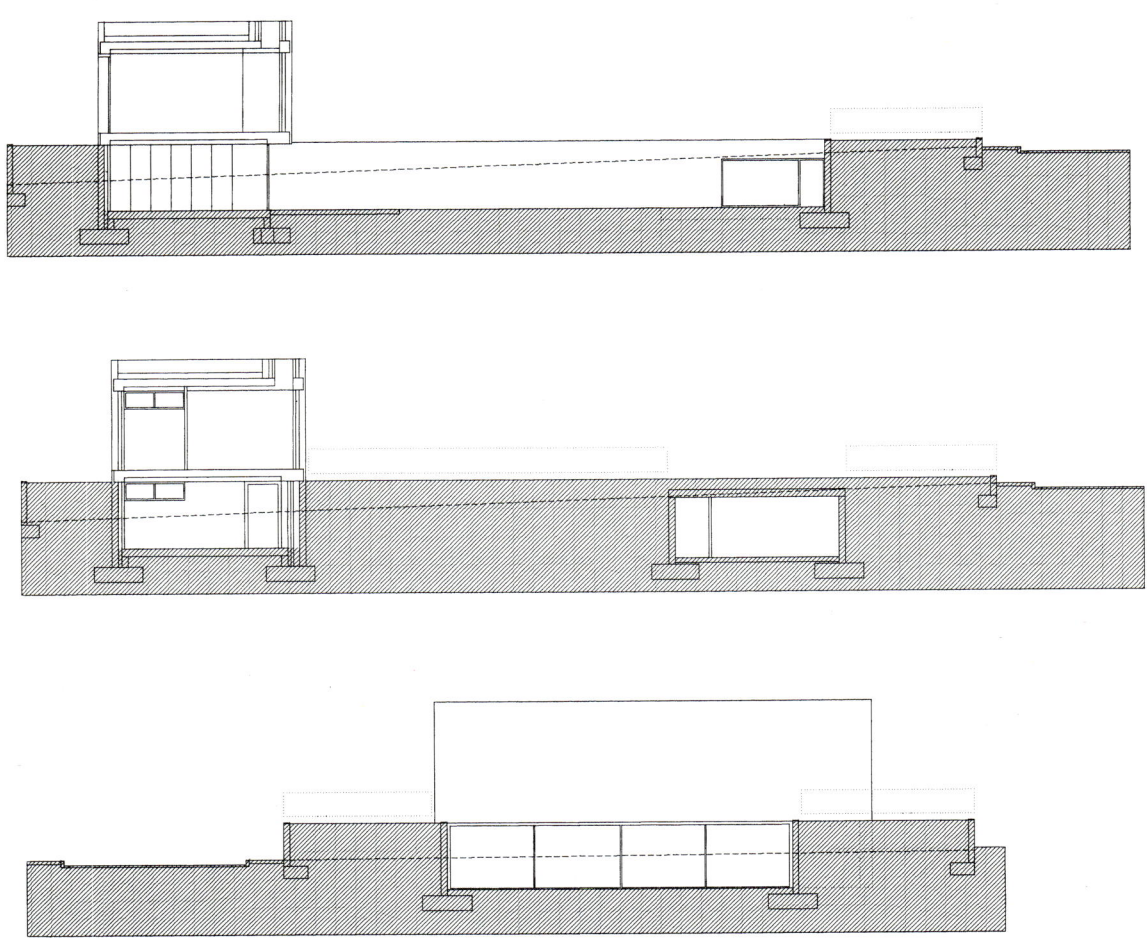

These young architects have managed to make the most of somewhat unattractive surroundings and have provided the house with the necessary degree of privacy. On the other hand, the materials and finishes enhance the quality of the project as a simple, elegant residence.

Architects: Van Berkel + Bos / UN Studio
Location: Het Gooi, Holland
Construction date: 1998
Photographs: Christian Richters, Ingmar Swalue

The Möbius House is a new way of understanding a residence: the spaces succeed each other and no clear limits are established between rooms.

The absence of limits is not only physical, but applies to those limits affecting the function or temporality of activities that take place in the house. Van Berkel + Bos are the authors of a theoretical manifesto that materializes in this residence in Het Gooi, Holland. The building smoothly incorporates program, circulations and structure, with no "seams" showing. All the activities in the house are interrelated so that work and social, family and individual life find their niche in a spiral arrangement.

The plan includes two closed linear itineraries that come together in the zones of passage, showing how two people can live together while remaining independent, meeting in specific places or common living areas. The idea of two people living their own lives, but sharing certain moments, even exchanging roles at certain times, has impacted the way the house has been materialized and constructed.

The structure of movement also affects the organization of the two basic materials used for building: concrete and glass. Concrete is used in the construction of furniture; the facades and a number of interior partitions are made of glass.

The two closed itineraries compose the skeleton of the building's formal organization. This diagrammatic architecture is a process of liberation: the scheme frees the architecture from language, interpretation and meaning. The diagram's abstract nature makes it possible to work with only two materials, while the house's around-the-clock use conditioned the layout. The arrangement of the two closed itineraries acquires a space-time dimension applied 24 hours a day to the family life that takes place in the house.

Although the mathematical model is not literally applied to the building, it is conceptualized, and can be found in some of the architectural ingredients: in the light, the stairs, and in the way the occupants move through the house. In this way, the Möbius diagram introduces aspects of itinerary and durability. It has been incorporated into the building only after having undergone mutation in order to become "buildable."

In the case of the Möbius House, the housing type is used as a privileged field of experimentation in which to observe end-of-the-century domestic dreams. In this sense, the project is a clear manifestation of the theories developed by this Dutch team, who have managed to create an astonishing building that contains environments that relate form, function and time while creating warm, sophisticated atmospheres.

Möbius House

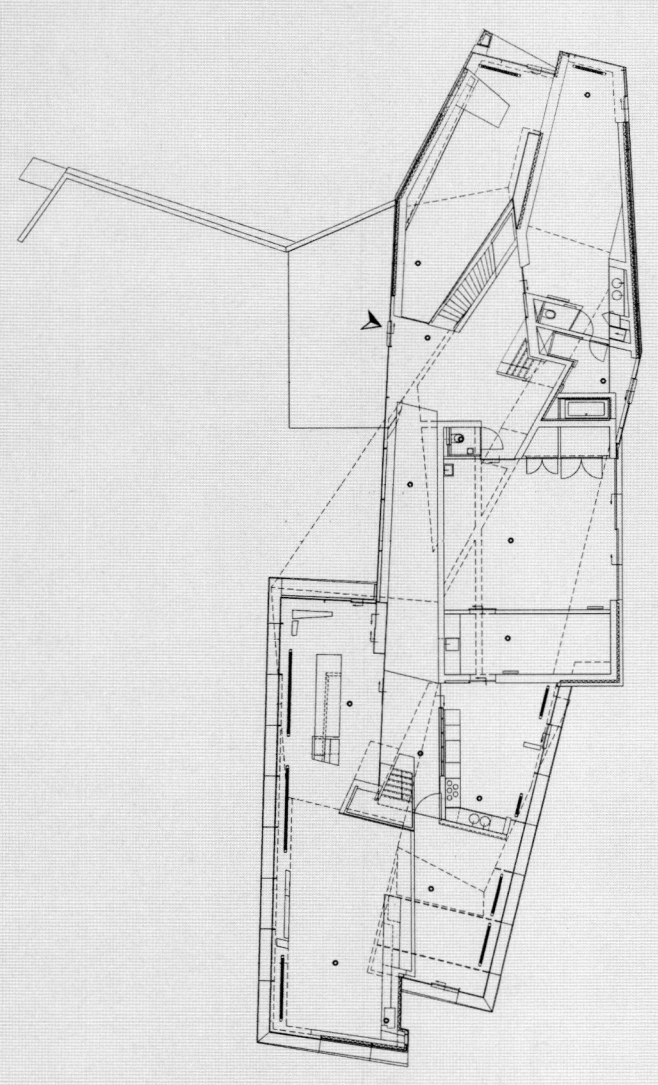
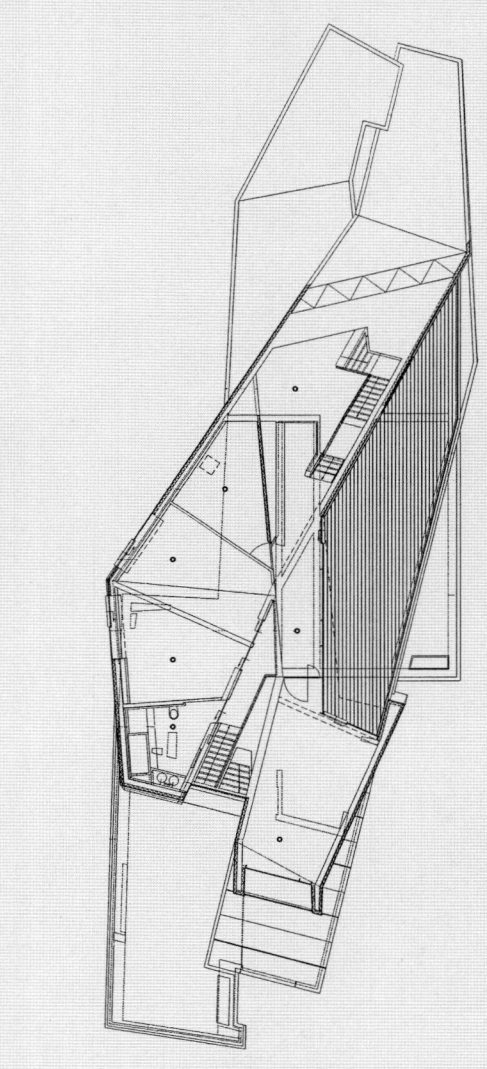

The house's program obeys an atypical distribution. There is a direct relationship between spaces and activities carried out during an entire day. Consequently, the rooms succeed each other as in a time sequence.

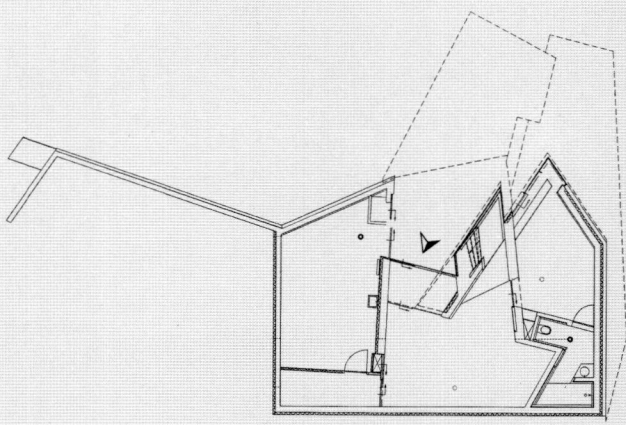

The basic materials are bare concrete and glass, which exchange roles in a number of situations. Glass constitutes part of the facades and some of the interior partitions, while several pieces of furniture are made of concrete.

Following page: UN Studio hired a specialist to depict the spaces being used, from a spectator's point of view. The house cannot be perceived in its entirety if it is understood only as a construction. Use and itineraries are integral parts of the project.

Möbius House

Architects: Kazuyo Sejima and Ryue Nishizawa
Location: Tokyo, Japan
Construction date: 1997
Photograhs: Shinkenchiku-Sha

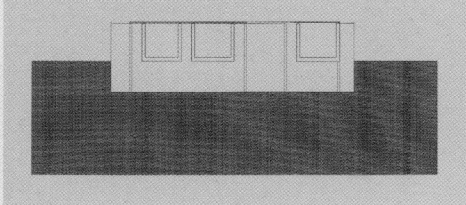

The M House is a fine example of the flexibility and expertise that characterize projects by this studio, which is headed by the Japanese architect Kazuyo Sejima. Two other qualities that typify the residence are originality and freshness.

The house is located in a high-class residential quarter of downtown Tokyo, whose density is increasing due to the subdivision of building land into plots — like that of the M House — of 2,150 square feet.

The site is bordered to the south by the street and on the other three sides by adjacent buildings. To obtain privacy, many of the homeowners overlooking the street have had to build walls and draw curtains. Given this paradox — having to close what was originally intended to be open — the designers of the M House decided that two fundamental aspects of the project would be harmony with the surroundings and the guarantee of privacy.

The mechanism applied to meet these criteria is a sunken patio that illuminates and ventilates the floor below ground, while connecting it to the floor above, the street and the sky. The street-level floor is divided crosswise by corridors, stairs and the patio. It contains those parts of the house whose function requires independence, such as the garage, the double bedroom, and the guest room.

The floor below, a more unified space, is arranged around the patio and characterized by ease of movement from one part to another. The kitchen, dining room and studio are also located on this floor.

One of the main virtues of this house is that it is made-to-measure for the owners, a young couple, both of whom work. Two studios, several bathrooms and room for two cars provide privacy and independence. Furthermore, after conversations between the clients and architects, it became clear that a party room was necessary, since the couple entertains often as part of their jobs. Provision was also made for the possibility of children in the future. The homogeneous space of the M House is the outcome of many factors, including the architects' work on the program requirements, everyday needs protection from the surrounding environment, and the pursuit of light, air and privacy. The complex process of condensing these functions led to a formal, astoundingly simple, result.

Clarity and nakedness, products of an abstract way of designing the house, are perfectly reflected in the plans and are present in all the different environments, from the facades to the treatment of the interiors.

The M House has been designed with an admirable combination of sensitivity and intelligence. The result, a home of truly impressive beauty, confirms the fact that Kazuyo Sejima and Ryue Nishizawa belong to the host of Japanese architects who strive to shake off inherited prejudices in order to find solutions to the conflicts of contemporary society.

M House

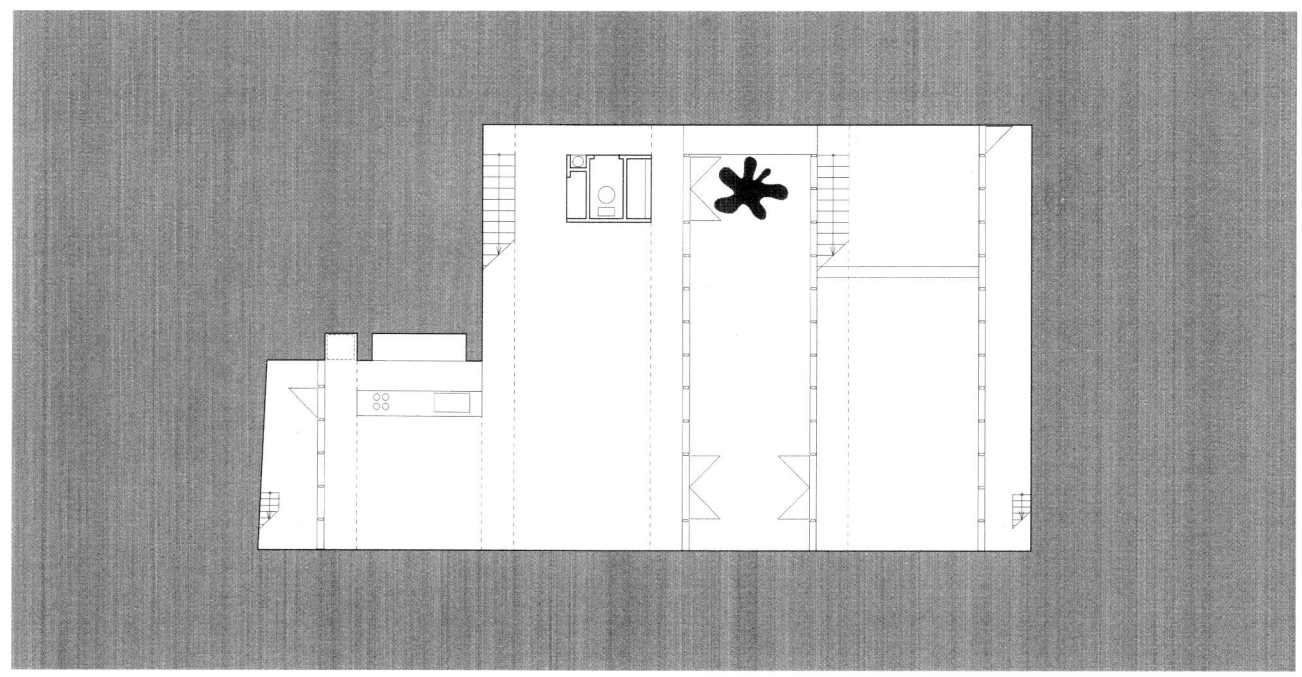

The basement accommodates the dining room, studios, living rooms, and open-air patios. The ground floor, at street level, contains the main bedroom, guest room and the garage.

The strategy adopted by Sejima and Nishizawa involved hollowing out the ground in order to open the house to the exterior without sacrificing privacy.

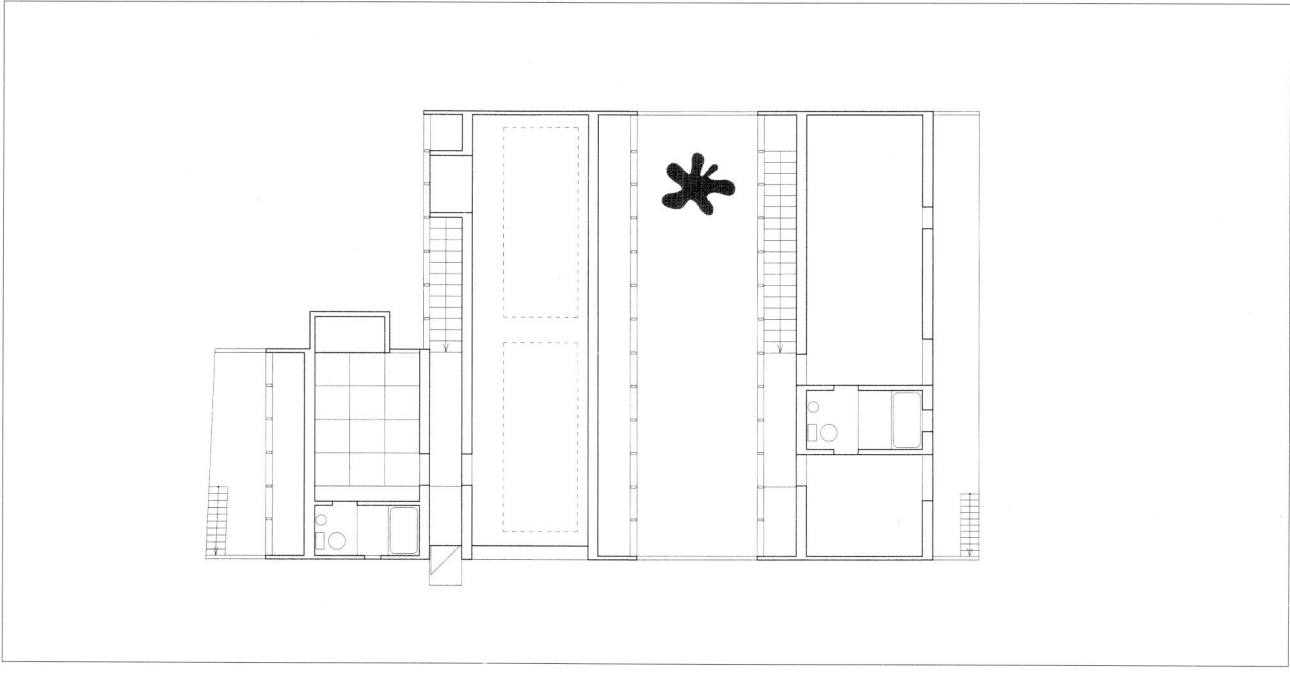

The functional program was clear and had to include large, flexible spaces in which to accommodate different activities: workstudios, party room and so on. The adjacent photograph shows the patio, which links the house directly to the exterior.

After the "house in the woods" and the S House, these Japanese architectshave astonished us once again with a magnificent minimalist environment. A sober, luminous and highly elegant residence resulted from their choice of light materials and careful consideration of constructional details.